MAGNIFICENCE
ONSTAGE AT THE MET

Set design by Jean-Pierre Ponnelle for Mozart's *Idomeneo*, 1982

ROBERT JACOBSON

MAGNIFICENCE ONSTAGE AT THE MET

TWENTY GREAT OPERA PRODUCTIONS

PHOTO EDITOR:
GERALD FITZGERALD

With 274 illustrations,
117 in color

SIMON AND SCHUSTER · NEW YORK
THE METROPOLITAN OPERA GUILD

Acknowledgments

The texts of the individual chapters devoted to the twenty productions discussed in this book have benefited greatly in that the author has been able to draw on interviews granted by the various distinguished directors, designers, and conductors at the time of the original staging of each work. Such quotations help to provide a sense of immediacy and involvement in the creation of each new staging, and the author expresses his special gratitude to August Everding, Nathaniel Merrill, Tanya Moiseiwitsch, Desmond Heeley, Robert O'Hearn, Jean-Pierre Ponnelle, and Sandro Sequi for the time and personal interest they lent this project.

Thanks are also owed to colleagues for their invaluable help in the preparation of the manuscript: Jean Uppman, who compiled the performance history of each of the works featured: Robert A. Tuggle, Archivist of the Metropolitan Opera; and Dorothy A. Kauffman, Editorial Assistant of *Opera News*. We are grateful, too, for the generosity of the gifted photographers who made their work available—Beth Bergman, Erika Davidson, Johan Elbers, and James Hefferman, together with his most gracious associate Winnie Klotz. The photographic illustrations are supplemented by original designs for stage sets and costumes, and we thank Roger Gross, Desmond Heeley, Rubén de Saavedra, and Robert L. B. Tobin for lending valuable designer artwork. Greatly appreciated as well is the cooperation of JoAnn Forman and Clarie Freimann in allowing us the freedom of the photographic files of the Metropolitan Opera Guild's Education Department. Finally, thanks are due to the instigator and prime mover of this project, Roland Gelatt, whose constant encouragement did so much to ensure its realization, a task in which his colleagues at Thames and Hudson—editors Stanley Baron and Mark Trowbridge, and designer Ian Mackenzie-Kerr—contributed their various skills.

This publication was conceived and created by
The Metropolitan Opera Guild in collaboration with
Thames and Hudson, Ltd.

© 1985 Thames and Hudson, Ltd., London

Published by Simon and Schuster
A Division of Simon & Schuster, Inc.
Simon and Schuster Building
Rockefeller Center
1230 Avenue of the Americas
New York, New York 10020
SIMON AND SCHUSTER and colophon are registered
trademarks of Simon & Schuster, Inc.

1 2 3 4 5 6 7 8 9 10

Library of Congress Cataloging in Publication Data

Jacobson, Robert M.
    Magnificence: onstage at the Met.

    Includes index.
    1. Opera—New York (N.Y.) 2. Metropolitan Opera
(New York, N.Y.) I. Title.
ML1711.8.N3M435   1985   782.1'07'3097471   85-2321
ISBN 0-671-55723-8

Printed and bound in Japan by Dai Nippon

Contents

Introduction: Onstage at the Old Met, 1883–1966   7

La Bohème   16
Zeffirelli/Zeffirelli/Hall/Wechsler

Boris Godunov   28
Everding/Lee/Hall

Cavalleria Rusticana/Pagliacci   40
Zeffirelli/Zeffirelli

Les Contes d'Hoffmann   56
Schenk/Schneider-Siemssen/Frey/Wechsler

Falstaff   68
Zeffirelli/Zeffirelli

Fidelio   80
Schenk/Aronson

Francesca da Rimini   88
Faggioni/Frigerio/Squarciapino/Wechsler

Die Frau ohne Schatten   100
Merrill/O'Hearn

Idomeneo   112
Ponnelle/Ponnelle/Wechsler

L'Italiana in Algeri   124
Ponnelle/Ponnelle

Lulu   132
Dexter/Herbert/Wechsler

Manon Lescaut   144
Menotti/Heeley/Wechsler

Otello   152
Zeffirelli/Zeffirelli/Hall

Parade: An Evening of French Music Theatre   164
Dexter/Hockney/Wechsler

Peter Grimes   176
Guthrie/Moiseiwitsch

Porgy and Bess   188
Merrill/O'Hearn/Wechsler

I Puritani   200
Sequi/Lee/Hall

Tannhäuser   212
Schenk/Schneider-Siemssen/Zipprodt/Wechsler

Tristan und Isolde   224
Everding/Schneider-Siemssen

Die Zauberflöte   236
Rennert/Chagall

Performance history   248

Sources of illustrations   255

Index   256

Introduction: Onstage at the Old Met, 1883–1966

LIKE ANY OTHER flourishing art form, opera—with its grand mixture of music, theater, voice, and spectacle—constantly undergoes periodic cycles, and the style of production at the Metropolitan Opera House is no exception to this general rule. In operatic terms, the epoch around the turn of the century may well be regarded as the age of the singer. Later, with the coming of Gustav Mahler and Arturo Toscanini, opera could be said to have entered the age of the conductor. And the period since World War II may well be dubbed the age of the director, designer or that recent phenomenon, the director-designer. Today, we are inclined, for better or for worse, to refer to "Zeffirelli's *La Bohème*," "Ponnelle's *Idomeneo*" or "Everding's *Tristan und Isolde*." Of course the operas remain the creations of Puccini, Mozart, and Wagner respectively, but they have undergone complete dramatic and visual rethinking and reworking by the director and the designer. The advent of talking films since the late 1920s and of television since the late 1940s has made a great difference to people's perception of opera as a visual experience, as compared with the attitudes of a half-century earlier. Voice, voice, and more voice seemed to be the standard when the opera house first opened its doors in 1883—voice and individual personalities, along with acting ability and charisma; but as far as production values went, vast painted drops full of ornate, picture-postcard detail and elaborate costumes appeared to be the order of the day. The concept of a theatrical unity, a total vision, was far from the minds of those who ran the Met and those who sat in the glittering gilt auditorium.

A look at the opening-night program for Gounod's *Faust*, on October 22, 1883, reveals these credits: "The Scenery by Messrs. Fox, Schaeffer, Maeder, and Thompson. The costumes are entirely new, and were manufactured at Venice by D. Ascoli." Cast and conductor are given appropriate billing, but as for mention of a stage director—there is none. In fact, there is no record of a "stage director" listed on a printed program until the opening night of 1917–18, when Richard Ordynski was on hand to direct Verdi's *Aida*, although he had taken charge of DeKoven's *The Canterbury Pilgrims* a year earlier. Before Giulio Gatti-Casazza created the position of "stage director" for Ordynski, only the term "stage manager" could be seen, and one presumes this person told the artists where to enter and exit, to walk, sit, and stand in the physical settings as they existed; and this manager had to cope with the wishes of this or that soprano, tenor or bass as to how to play any given role to its greatest effect. The demand for opera as a mighty unified art form had yet to dawn, at least in America.

At the time Gatti took command of the Metropolitan in 1908, numerous productions were deemed shabby and poorly executed. The *New York Times* critic, Richard Aldrich, set the record straight in 1900, writing, "Habitués of the Metropolitan Opera House have been called upon to suffer many things to compensate for the privilege of listening to

Set designed by Mariano Fortuny for Act I of Wagner's *Tristan und Isolde*, 1909–10; and Willy Pogany's design for the shipwreck scene in Act I of Rossini's *L'Italiana in Algeri*, 1919–20.

Opposite

Design by Angelo Parravicini for Act IV, Scene 2, the Tomb Scene, of Verdi's *Aida*, 1923–24; the sets for this production—one of the most popular of the Gatti era—remained in use until 1950.

Stage designs of the Gatti era: (*top*) by Serge Soudeikine for Stravinsky's *Le Rossignol*, 1925–26; (*center*) by Robert Edmond Jones for John Alden Carpenter's ballet *Skyscrapers*, 1926–27; and by Jo Mielziner for Louis Gruenberg's *The Emperor Jones*, 1932–33.

Opposite

Two designs by Joseph Urban: for the final scene of Halévy's *La Juive*—the boiling cauldron into which the heroine is thrown, 1919–20; and (*below*) for the Garden Scene in Act III of Gounod's *Faust*, 1917–18, a production which originally starred Geraldine Farrar as Marguerite, and which was retained for more than three decades.

their great singers—incompetent and inane stage management, miserable and inappropriate scenery and costumes, a chorus wretched in vocal equipment and squalid in appearance." Yet in this desert there had to have been the occasional oasis. In 1900–01, the third season of Maurice Grau's regime, a staging of Reyer's *Salammbô* was called the most expensive he had yet offered; the sets for this production had been copied by a staff artist, Homer F. Emens, from the Paris Opéra originals. Earlier, during the seasons of German opera initiated by Leopold Damrosch and carried out by Edmund Stanton, the productions accumulated by Henry E. Abbey in the Met's first season were used, and for the Wagner operas there were duplicates of those used at Bayreuth, designed and created under the composer's own eye, and on occasion even directed by two Wagner disciples, Wilhelm Hock and Anton Fuchs. With Abbey's return in 1891, the sets and costumes of the last decade of the century were thought to be magnificent, as befitting this Golden Age. At the outset of Heinrich Conried's regime, in 1903, the Met rebuilt its stage for a special production, the first staged presentation of *Parsifal* outside Bayreuth, and for Mahler's *Tristan und Isolde* in 1907–08, sets and costumes were imported from La Scala. In that same season the famous sets and costumes for *Fidelio* by the Vienna Secessionist Alfred Roller were duplicated. Most productions, however, with their realistically painted drops (some serving for any number of castles, fortresses, and ornate ballrooms), emerged as serviceably drab, or drably serviceable.

Yet much was happening on the European front: for example, such modern visionaries as Adolphe Appia and Edward Gordon Craig wanted to strip opera and theater of this rigid tyranny of realism by using light and simplified sculptural forms; and a new synthesis was being effected by Sergei Diaghilev, who elevated the aesthetic relationship between painter, choreographer-director, composer, and librettist to the highest plane. With Gatti's arrival at the Met in 1908, a new air of theatricality was virtually inevitable, while the simultaneous arrival of Arturo Toscanini helped clean up musical matters as well. Gatti noted at the time that "a large part of the scenery [is] so much worn or in such poor taste as not to be of any further use." It is said that when he toured the 40th Street warehouse, he found one set representing an ugly court with a door to the rear opening up on the sea. Asking what it was, he was told that it had been used interchangeably for Acts I of Ambroise Thomas's *Mignon* and Verdi's *Otello!* As with his historic opening *Aida* (designed by Mario Sala and Angelo Parravicini), Gatti sought and obtained new or refurbished sets for the theater he would guide for the next twenty-seven years. From Vienna he imported designer Hans Kautsky, who began with *Die Zauberflöte* in 1912–13 (the critic W.J. Henderson called it "without question the finest spectacle . . . the lyric drama has known here"), a new *Ring* cycle in 1913–14 (some of this was to last until as late as 1948), as well as Korngold's *Die tote Stadt*, Strauss's *Der Rosenkavalier* (after Roller's originals), Wagner's *Tannhäuser*, and other works in the early 1920s.

For the 1909–10 season Mariano Fortuny designed a new *Tristan und Isolde*, while Paul Paquereau was responsible in that same season for Gluck's *Orfeo ed Euridice* and, in 1910–11, *Armide*—both under Toscanini. Antonio Rovescalli designed a number of productions, beginning with Massenet's *Manon*, in 1908–09, going on to Franchetti's *Germania*, the world premiere of Granados's *Goyescas*, and Wolf-Ferrari's *I Gioielli della Madonna*, occasionally in collaboration with Vittorio Rota. In the case of a sensational new *Aida* in 1923–24, Rovescalli and Rota executed

Set design by Donald Oenslager for Strauss's *Salome*, 1933–34, the penultimate season of the Gatti era.

Notable designs of the Johnson era: by Paul Tchelitchev for Gluck's *Orfeo ed Euridice*, 1935–36, a production by George Balanchine, with dancers onstage and singers in the pit; and by Mstislav Dobujinsky for the Gallows Scene in Act II of Verdi's *Un Ballo in maschera*, the opera which opened the 1940–41 season.

designs by Parravicini and Sala, which lasted twenty-eight seasons. Parravicini was also responsible for the Met premiere of Verdi's *Simon Boccanegra* in 1931–32. With Gluck's *Iphigenia in Taurus* in 1916–17, J. Monroe Hewlett, Charles Bosing, and A.T. Hewlett became the first American designers to see their work on the Met stage, while James Fox that same season furnished designs for *The Canterbury Tales*, Donizetti's *L'Elisir d'amore*, and Delibes's *Lakmé*. Otherwise, there were more Europeans: Giovanni Grandi from La Scala and Hans Peuhringer from Vienna.

With his penchant for Russian opera, Gatti brought in designers ideally suited to visualize them. In 1912–13, the Alexander Golovine-Alexandre Benois staging of *Boris Godunov* (first produced in 1908 in Paris by Diaghilev) was brought to the Met and used until the late 1930s, when the sets were repainted and reworked for further use. Willy Pogany designed Rimsky-Korsakov's *Le Coq d'or*, celebrated as one of the most colorful productions of the Gatti era, and Rossini's *L'Italiana in Algeri*. Serge Soudeikine made his Met debut with an authentic, spectacular *Petrouchka*, and went on to tackle Stravinsky's *Le Rossignol*, as well as *Die Zauberflöte*, *Mignon*, *Sadko*, *Der fliegende Holländer*, and *The Fair at Sorochintsky* (1930–31). Another Russian émigré, Boris Anisfeld, brought what the *Sun* called "the blazing brush" to the exotica of Leroux's *La Reine Fiammette* (1918–19), later doing the same for Wolff's *L'Oiseau bleu* (dubbed more "opulent" than any production the Met had previously offered), Boito's *Mefistofele*, Rimsky's *Snegurochka*, and Massenet's *Le Roi de Lahore* (1923–24).

But it was the hand of the Viennese designer Joseph Urban that dominated the Gatti era until 1932–33, with some fifty-three productions that combined his superb theatricality in any number of styles (realistic, abstract, symbolic) with his rich architectural sets and new Continental painting techniques involving pointillistic textures to be used with sophisticated lighting. This was the closest the Met got to the concept of total theater initiated by Appia and others, and many of Urban's creations endured well into the Bing era. The sets for his initial effort, *Faust* (1917–18), were commended as being "of great beauty, and of such design as to lend themselves to a complete shattering of the conventional stage business." His exceptional eye was brought to bear on such diverse works as Spontini's *La Vestale*, Wagner's *Parsifal*, Giordano's *La Cena delle beffe*, Meyerbeer's *L'Africaine*, Strauss's *Die aegyptische Helene*, Křenek's *Jonny spielt auf*, Bizet's *Carmen*, Offenbach's *Les Contes d'Hoffmann*, Verdi's *Falstaff*, Mozart's *Così fan tutte* (New York's first), Humperdinck's *Hänsel und Gretel*, Halévy's *La Juive*, Weinberger's *Schwanda*, Massenet's *Thaïs*, Suppé's *Boccaccio*, Taylor's *The King's Henchman* and *Peter Ibbetson*, and the U.S. premiere of Puccini's *Turandot*. One wonders how those beautiful sketches would translate to the stage today, with all our modern lighting techniques.

Also of lasting value, if of lesser inspiration, was the work of Joseph Novak, a scenic painter who first came to attention with his designs for *Cavalleria rusticana*/*Pagliacci* (1923–24). Novak remained at the Met as a staff painter until 1950, creating productions for Alfano's *Madonna Imperia*, Ravel's *L'Heure espagnole*, Smetana's *The Bartered Bride*, Mascagni's *Iris*, Montemezzi's *La Notte di Zoraima*, and, in 1948–49, Britten's *Peter Grimes*.

For a number of years, Gatti had as his "stage managers" (to take care of stage direction) Jules Speck for the Italian and French repertories and Anton Schertel for the German. Wilhelm Von Wymetal came in 1922, and subsequently worked in the house intermittently until 1936; he was particularly adept at getting an opera onstage in just a few hours. In essence, the director's function was basically to tell people where to stand, while conductors insisted that singers be placed where they could see them best. But there were exceptions. Playwright David Belasco came to supervise the two Puccini operas based on his plays—*Madama Butterfly* in 1907 and *La Fanciulla del West* in 1910. He did the same for Leoncavallo's *Zaza* in 1919–20, and gave the three works a vivid theatrical life by encouraging his artists to act their roles as well as sing.

By the late 1920s, Gatti may have felt the German theaters had a point with their new emphasis on the *régisseur*. Accordingly, he engaged Ernst Lert, who had worked with Toscanini at La Scala, to improve the dramatic qualities of the repertory. Previously, the Met had been putting new productions onstage with almost no rehearsal, but now Gatti allowed the director a maximum of three or four sessions, representing ten to twelve hours' rehearsal time, even for the most elaborate of productions. Lert began in 1929–30 with *Fanciulla* (designed by Novak), and with Lattuada's *Le Preziose ridicole* the next season he was felt to be imaginative and above the Met average of the time. Still, this was the period of the Depression, and financially the theater was fighting for its life. Lert left after these two seasons (to be replaced by Alexander Sanine), declaring, "It is not opera that is dying, only the traditional method of presenting it." In 1935 he broadened his angry criticisms to include the Met's "lack of co-ordination" that made the results more of a variety show—despite the efforts of an experienced impresario, lavishly paid conductors, the most highly publicized stars, the most elaborate scenic artists. As director, Lert had been placed "in an impossible situation," being named as "responsible for the production," even though Gatti had not granted him a single rehearsal "for nineteen out of twenty such productions."

Before his departure in 1935, Gatti had also made a bid for the new American stagecraft as represented in Robert Edmond Jones with his "modernistic" scenery for Carpenter's ballet *Skyscrapers* (1925–26), Norman Bel Geddes for Breil's *The Legend*, Cadman's *Shanewis* and Hadley's *Cleopatra's Night*, and Jo Mielziner for Gruenberg's *The Emperor Jones*. Gatti's successor, Herbert Witherspoon, had planned to spend money on stage direction, casting an eye about for the German-based Caspar Neher and Carl Ebert or Heinz Tietjen and Lothar Wallerstein. As a result of Witherspoon's sudden death before taking office, former tenor Edward Johnson became general manager. Irving Kolodin noted, "Little had been done to restore the visual elements of the Met's productions to a respectable level . . . there had been little attempt to do the staggering job of restoration on the scenery for the standard repertory bequeathed to Johnson by Gatti." Despite a rather undistinguished period for scenic and theatrical standards—the result of the problems of money and materials brought on by the Depression and the war—what Johnson did do was to bring in Herbert Graf to establish stage discipline, beginning with the 1936–37 season. Graf had studied with Roller in Vienna and had worked with Toscanini on *Die Meistersinger* at Salzburg. His Met career began with a staging of Saint-Saëns' *Samson et Dalila* (Henderson called Act I "one of the most memorable achievements of the Metropolitan") and came to include *Falstaff*, *Orfeo ed Euridice*, *Le Nozze di Figaro*, *Un Ballo in maschera*, and *Alceste*, the latter designed by Richard Rychtarik. During the first dozen years of the Rudolf Bing regime, Graf would serve as director for four memorable productions designed by Eugene Berman. Johnson also hired

Three designs of the 1940s: (*top*) by Richard Rychtarik for Act I, Scene 1, of Mozart's *Die Zauberflöte*, 1941–42, a production directed by Herbert Graf and conducted by Bruno Walter; (*center*) by Lee Simonson for Act III, Scene 1, of Wagner's *Götterdämmerung*, a concept that resembles the valley of the Hudson more than that of the Rhine, 1947–48; and by H. M. Křehan-Crayon for Act I of Puccini's *Manon Lescaut*, 1949–50, one of the last productions of the Johnson era.

Set designs of the Bing era: (*top*) by Rolf Gérard for Act I, inside the cloister of St. Just, of Verdi's *Don Carlo*, 1950–51; (*center*) by Caspar Neher for the Tavern Scene in Act II of Berg's *Wozzeck*, a Met premiere in 1958–59; and by Cecil Beaton for Act I, outside the palace in Peking, of Puccini's *Turandot*, 1960–61.

Opposite

Designs by Eugene Berman for the 1957–58 production of Mozart's *Don Giovanni*, staged by Herbert Graf and conducted by Karl Böhm, who was making his Met debut: (*above*) a backdrop of a castle in Seville; (*below, left*) a costume design for Don Giovanni; and a sketch for the scene between Donna Anna and Don Ottavio.

Graf's pupil, Dino Yannopoulos, whose contributions began with *Il Tabarro* in 1945–46 and continued well into the Bing era with *Andrea Chénier, Don Pasquale, Ernani,* and the revival of *Norma* in 1956 for Maria Callas, who was making her Met debut.

Johnson called on Lothar Wallerstein, who had been chief *régisseur* in Vienna, to set up some pre-season acting classes for the young, inexperienced artists Johnson engaged, coaching them intensively in their new roles. Also on the scene was the all-purpose Désiré Defrère, beginning 1934–35, as well as Leopold Sachse for the Wagner works. In design, Donald Oenslager, who had made a big impression with his three-dimensional, completely built (no drops) *Salome* in the Johnson era, took on *Otello* and *The Abduction from the Seraglio*, while Rychtarik looked after *Alceste, Die Zauberflöte, Phoebus and Pan, The Island God,* and *Lucia di Lammermoor,* before being appointed to the new post of co-ordinator of stage matters in 1947–48. Russian émigré Mstislav Dobujinsky supplied an ornate *Un Ballo in maschera* (1940–41) and Johnson's last production, Mussorgsky's *Khovanshchina* in 1949–50, some of the sets for which went into a revised *Boris Godunov* in 1952–53. Jonel Jorgulesco created *La Traviata* in 1934–35 and *Le Nozze di Figaro* in 1939–40, and Paul Tchelitchev collaborated with George Balanchine on a forward-looking, though ill-received, *Orfeo ed Euridice* in 1935–36. For Rogers's *The Warrior* (1946–47) Samuel Leve provided the company's first projected scenery, and in 1948 Lee Simonson came up with the most ambitious scenic project in two decades, an ill-conceived *Ring* cycle that took the Hudson River and Valley as its inspiration, but there was H.M. Křehan-Crayon's lovely *Manon Lescaut* as compensation.

When Rudolf Bing first came to the Met, it was from the distinctly European milieu of Darmstadt and Berlin's Städtische Oper, followed by Glyndebourne and Edinburgh—all places where new developments, in terms of treating opera as theater, were occurring. Throughout the 1920s and 1930s the German houses had played a pioneering role, by adopting a fiercely dramatic approach to opera; and just after World War II, with major singers in short supply, the European companies took to emphasizing dramatic values with a vengeance. Bing launched his long tenure with a favorite work, Verdi's *Don Carlo,* and called on Rolf Gérard (a colleague from his Glyndebourne years) for the design and the well-known Shakespearean specialist Margaret Webster, who thus became the company's first woman director. This *Don Carlo* proved to be a revelation in terms of honoring every aspect of opera, and Bing was instantly hailed as the man who was bringing the Met into the twentieth century with "a sense of style long absent from this stage." Bing began a program of replacing or repairing badly dilapidated productions in a rather barren scenic cupboard, as well as improving the entire visual aspect so that the stage picture would be in harmony with its sounds.

Despite a number of flops, the twenty-two-year Bing regime proved to be one of expanding theatrical boundaries, often reflecting a taste for the Broadway "fashionable." In his first years be brought in such theater people as Garson Kanin for *Fledermaus,* Alfred Lunt for *Così fan tutte,* Tyrone Guthrie for *Carmen,* Joseph L. Mankiewicz for *La Bohème,* Balanchine for *The Rake's Progress,* Peter Brook for Gounod's *Faust* (a *cause célèbre* because the action was reset in time—in the nineteenth century, the period in which the opera was composed) and *Eugene Onegin,* José Quintero for *Cavalleria/Pagliacci,* and many others. Later would come the actor/director Cyril Ritchard (*Il Barbiere di Siviglia* and *Figaro,* as well as *Hoffmann* and *La*

Other set designs of the Bing era: (*top*) by Harry Horner for Act II, Scene 2, of Mozart's *Die Zauberflöte*, 1955–56; (*center*) by Horace Armistead for Leoncavallo's *Pagliacci*, 1950–51; by Teo Otto for Act I of Wagner's *Tristan und Isolde*, 1959–60; and (*right*) by Motohiro Nagasaka for Act I of Puccini's *Madama Butterfly*, 1957–58.

Périchole) and Jean-Louis Barrault (*Faust* for the farewell year on 39th Street). Bing engaged the composer Gian Carlo Menotti to direct Barber's *Vanessa* and his own *The Last Savage* (which introduced the brilliant designs of Beni Montresor), Yoshio Aoyama for an authentic *Madama Butterfly* (designed by Motohiro Nagasaka), Margarita Wallmann for *Lucia di Lammermoor* and *La Gioconda*, and in 1964 Franco Zeffirelli with *Falstaff*, thus marking the beginning of his long association with the Met.

From Bing's own past came Carl Ebert, who with Caspar Neher had created a sensation in Berlin a quarter of a century earlier with their expressionistic *Macbeth* as part of the German Verdi revival (by 1959 it was found to be dated). Ebert was to tackle *Martha* and *Ariadne auf Naxos*, while Neher brought his staging of Berg's *Wozzeck*, with its strong 1920s overtones, under Herbert Graf's direction. Also from the German theatrical scene came Günther Rennert, first in 1960–61 for *Nabucco* and later for *Un Ballo in maschera* and *Manon*, but he was more at home with *Salome* and *Die Zauberflöte*. Nathaniel Merrill, who began as a young staff director, emerged on his own in 1961 with *L'Elisir d'amore*, collaborating with Robert O'Hearn, who gained some notoriety by having Dulcamara arrive by gas balloon. That team remained a constant until Bing's retirement, and returned in the 1984–85 season with *Porgy and Bess*. Among designers, Gérard emerged as Bing's regular creator through the 1960s, working on operas ranging from *Fledermaus* and *Aida* to *Arabella*, *Eugene Onegin*, and *La Sonnambula*—nineteen productions in all. Thus Gérard became to Bing what Urban had been to Gatti, although with far fewer productions. But it was the exceptional Russian-born artist Eugene Berman who was to lend special distinction to this era with his sumptuous, Renaissance- and neo-baroque-inspired painterly fantasies for *Rigoletto*, *La Forza del destino*, *Il Barbiere di Siviglia*, *Don Giovanni*, and *Otello*; his *Don Giovanni* of 1957–58 was judged to be more organized and integrated than anything before at the Met. Bing had also installed new lighting to illuminate his designers' work, with backstage equipment as well as front lighting from masked installations in the auditorium. From the ranks came Charles Elson (who also undertook the stripping away of older productions and utilizing existing physical materials for rebuilt, repainted "semi-new" productions), Esteban Frances, Frederic Fox, Harry Horner, Ita Maximowna, Teo Otto, Wolfgang Roth (who gave the theater its first turntable with *Don Pasquale* in 1955–56), Oliver Smith (*La Traviata*, *Martha*),

Horace Armistead (a roundly condemned "modern" *Cav/Pag* in 1950–51, *The Rake's Progress* in 1952–53), Cecil Beaton (*Vanessa, Turandot, La Traviata*), Attilio Colonnello (*Lucia, Il Trovatore, Luisa Miller*), Oliver Messel (his Glyndebourne *Figaro* and *Ariadne* expanded and enlarged for the Met stage), Jacques Dupont (*Faust, Carmen*), and the young Rudolf Heinrich, who made a big impression with his brooding, neo-Expressionistic *Salome* (1964–65), then *Elektra* (1966–67)—offset by a disastrous *Der Freischütz* (1971–72).

The theatrical aspect of opera arrived and flourished during the Bing years. But although Bing ventured into a variety of stylistic areas, the values the Met came to stand for were much the same as those that prevailed when the opera house first opened in 1883: solid, traditional productions that would have a lasting life in the repertory. This is what the theater and its public seem to thrive on, no matter what the era. In fact, the Met has rarely ventured into the experimental or avant-garde in staging opera; given its repertory system, involving as it does constant cast changes, revivals, and tours, such an approach would have little chance of survival. More often than not, the theater added to its stock of productions the kind of sets (and staging) that endure over the years. In its way, Zeffirelli's massive, beautiful *Falstaff* of 1964–65 was the precursor of a production style that would be possible more often from 1966–67 in the new opera house at Lincoln Center with all its technical advantages, despite the ever-rising costs that accompany such lavish presentation.

In making the choice of twenty works to be featured in this book, we looked over—with both the past and the present in mind, and taking into account the vagaries of taste and style over the years since the move—all productions during the successive directorships of the new house: Bing, Schuyler B. Chapin, and then Anthony A. Bliss, who worked in collaboration with music director James Levine and director of productions John Dexter. The works selected for inclusion represent the Metropolitan Opera at its best, its grandest, its most magnificent. They sum up the finest of the wide range of operatic activity that the Met has encompassed during the last two decades of its first century. These productions, covering the years since 1964, have given the theater the flavor it possesses today as it settles into its second century.

La Bohème

PUCCINI

Production: **Franco Zeffirelli**   Sets: **Franco Zeffirelli**
Costumes: **Peter J. Hall**   Lighting: **Gil Wechsler**

La Bohème

WHEN the curtain went up on Franco Zeffirelli's production of *La Bohème* on December 14, 1981—marking the director-designer's return to the Met for the first time in nearly ten years—it revealed perhaps the most spectacular and extravagant staging of Puccini's youthful opera in its nearly ninety-year history; this was certainly one of the most opulent events ever witnessed on the Met or any stage. The public greeted it rapturously, with ovations inspired by the first sight of every act, but the critics were divided on this expensive *Bohème*, many claiming that gigantism had overwhelmed the work and that Zeffirelli had diminished the opera's powers of direct psychological and physical communication.

One had to admit that in a few instances the principal singers did become lost in the vastness of the sets, but Zeffirelli intended this to happen: he sought to evoke a sense of the burgeoning French capital in the mid-nineteenth century as a backdrop against which the intense, individual dramas in the opera are played out. Perhaps he took his cue from the observation of Mosco Carner, Puccini's biographer, that "countless performances year in year out have blunted our ears to the fact that Puccini's is one of the most original creations for the lyrical stage and the first opera in history to achieve an almost perfect fusion of romantic and realistic elements with impressionist features."

This was only the second time that Zeffirelli had agreed to produce *La Bohème*, the first being at La

Scala in 1963, with Herbert von Karajan conducting and with Mirella Freni and Gianni Raimondi as Mimi and Rodolfo. The great triumph of that production led to its being replicated at the Salzburg Easter Festival and the Vienna State Opera, as well as being filmed for international distribution; it also subsequently toured to Tokyo, Montreal, and Washington, D.C. Those who had seen that *Bohème* knew they had experienced perhaps the definitive poetic vision of the opera and one of the most significant productions in the second half of the twentieth century. Having received such acclaim, Zeffirelli was reluctant to touch the work again, for he could not see how to improve on the success of his first production. But he finally accepted the Met's invitation when he realized that, with the aid of a revolving stage as impressive as the one the Lincoln Center theater possesses, he could fulfill ideas which had been in his head for a number of years.

"This new conception," he said, "brings out the fragility of the Bohemian group as against the large, gray French capital. While the garret is small and intimate, the public is treated to Parisian skies, roofs, chimneys, and balconies. When Benoit comes to collect the rent, the artists head for the balcony to hide, and when the little party takes place in the last act, before Musetta's arrival, they rush outside, jumping from roof to roof. I want to underline the helplessness and humanity of these nice young people lost in that large city."

"The second act," as he describes it, "is on several levels, with a realistic city square in the center and the Café Momus under the ramp. Here, as all the others leave following the crowd, Mimi and Rodolfo remain, oblivious of everything, suddenly in love. For the Barrière d'Enfer in the third act, I've imagined the time before the *grands boulevards* were built, a corner of Paris belonging to the poor, with snow falling and some trees in their winter desolation. Mimi comes down from the path with some difficulty and later hides behind the tavern. It's not so simple to dress Mimi as it might appear. She's the central character, yet she's a modest, unassuming person. I see her as a *petite bourgeoise*."

Everything Zeffirelli envisioned and eventually put onstage made sense both textually and musically, yet strong controversy was aroused by his cinematic, super-realistic approach, which sought to set the librettists' and composer's figures in a larger framework. Zeffirelli felt that he interpreted them best in his audacious first- and fourth-act sets, the very scenes that came under the heaviest critical fire because of his removing the central characters so far from audience contact, up and back from the stage apron. "But this is exactly what Puccini wanted!" insists the director-designer.

Above

Director Franco Zeffirelli with Teresa Stratas (Mimi) and José Carreras (Rodolfo) onstage during a rehearsal for Act I.

◁ *Overleaf*

Act I. The painter Marcello (Richard Stilwell) and the poet Rodolfo (José Carreras), cold, hungry, and penniless in their garret high above the rooftops of Paris; and (*inset*) the seamstress Mimi (Teresa Stratas) and Rodolfo, who fall in love.

"His dream was to have that—a little flying seventh heaven of a garret where these few kids are at the top of the world, looking down at the chimneys of the bourgeoisie below them. They're higher, and they come across to you because they're higher—they've been placed on such an altar. This spectacular *Bohème* is immensely intimate. The fourth act has been imagined and felt as an intimate, small thing, with discreet voices and beautiful acting. My fourth act shows the intimacy of my handling *when* the piece requires it."

Zeffirelli's extraordinary sense of human pageantry and atmosphere is apparent in Act II in the gargantuan set of the Latin Quarter, with its multiple levels. He believes this to be the hardest act to stage because of the libretto: "They spend hours in the first act saying how cold it is, how freezing, and then in the second act suddenly they're *al fresco* on the sidewalks of Paris. So I devised these levels, these areas, and you go back and forth." And, indeed, when the curtain rises,

the warm, glowing interior of the Café Momus is hidden by the vendors' carts, only to be revealed when the Bohemians enter the café for supper, followed by Musetta's arrival with Alcindoro.

If works such as *Otello* and *Turandot* call for extravagance and spectacle, in the minds of some the love story that is *La Bohème* does not. There are those critics who insisted that Puccini's opera is not about modern anomie or people lost in a vast gray city, that these were clichés imposed on a story which actually—and simply—celebrates a tight circle of friends who make a small community of their own. According to the dissenters, *La Bohème* is about different kinds of love, passionate and casual, in which Mimi's longing for beauty and friendship breaks through her physical weakness. Such tender, intimate emotions were felt to be distanced by the production's impersonality. Did not Puccini—who so identified with his characters, and particularly his heroines—want listeners to throb and sob along with them?

Act I. The Bohemians avoid paying the rent: Rodolfo (José Carreras), Schaunard (Allan Monk), the landlord Benoit (Italo Tajo), Marcello (Richard Stilwell), and Colline (James Morris).

Act II. The street outside the Café Momus on Christmas Eve, with (*above*) the Bohemians seated around their table—Marcello (Richard Stilwell), Rodolfo (José Carreras), Mimi (Teresa Stratas), Schaunard (Allan Monk), and Colline (James Morris). In the inset (*opposite*) the flirtatious Musetta (Renata Scotto) pretends her shoe pinches in order to get rid of her admirer, the old *roué* Alcindoro (Italo Tajo).

Act II, finale. Alcindoro (Renato Capecchi), with the new shoe he has brought for Musetta.

Yet Zeffirelli's exceptional eye and taste combined to make his dream of *La Bohème* work. It is massive in every respect—scale of production, beauty of theatrical vision, and grandeur of total concept. The attention to detail, the magical changing of light are irresistible. His properly scaled garret for the starving artists—for once it looks right and not like the Soho loft of an arrived artist blown up to fill the stage—seems to float over a sprawling, picturesque, silver-gray wintry city, the quarters properly crammed with the paraphernalia of a painter, poet, *et al.*, the nearby chimneys smoking above the tiled rooftops. One can almost feel the long climb of stairs to this leaky, drafty aerie. Meanwhile, imperceptibly, the moonlight begins to flood through the grimy windows just as the new-found lovers begin the duet "O soave fanciulla" that ends the first act. When we return there for the last act, it is early summer, the sky broiling hot, murky, yellowish; pots of geraniums struggle to survive on the balcony, where the Bohemians are seen romping before Mimi returns to them to die.

Act III conveys the wintry atmosphere at dawn near the gates of Paris, while giving the principals a focused but broad playing area: a hill of drifting snow between the upper road and the cozily lit tavern, its roof weighted with icicles. Above this, Mimi, small and pathetic in black against these bleak outskirts of Paris, can circle Rodolfo and Marcello as she looks down on them, and learns the truth about her illness. Zeffirelli's stage picture makes it apparent that this frail creature has no chance of surviving in such a world of ice, snow, and darkness. Shadowy figures with umbrellas come and go in the wintry morning, as does a priest with his students, and one can feel the spirit and atmosphere of the old Paris that existed before large parts of the city were rebuilt by Haussmann.

But it is Act II, set in the Latin Quarter, that captivates the eye. Designed on three levels with a warren of streets and alleys and tall, warmly illuminated apartment buildings, the stage setting contains a series of *coups de théâtre* that brings Christmas Eve in Paris vibrantly to life with all the rich colors of a painting by Delacroix—Musetta, in brilliant red, making her entrance with Alcindoro in a hansom cab drawn by a real horse; milling throngs on all levels and in constant motion, strolling, eating, buying, looking; finally, a platoon of soldiers marching down the stone steps to cap the spectacle—altogether some 280 people onstage. The lovers are swept into the rhythm of the city and its vivid Bohemian life, complete with a man on stilts, a gypsy trainer with his dancing bear, and a magical Parpignol with his toys. Zeffirelli's vision seems to lift the simple love story in Henri Murger's novel *Scènes de la vie de Boheme*, on which the libretto is based, into another dimension, making cinematic use of this stage to convey a realism and a sense of pulsating life that are overwhelming.

And if his principals occasionally get absorbed into the bigger picture, Zeffirelli craftily limns each one visually. Rodolfo is a scruffy, unshaven poet, intense about everything he does; Marcello a sensitive Romantic painter in slouch hat and cape; Colline a Rasputin-like philosopher with stringy hair and beard. Mimi, her hair parted in the middle, large shawl over her narrow shoulders, frail, nervous, has seemingly stepped out of a Daumier lithograph. With her dark-circled eyes and caved-in demeanor, this Mimi comes to the garret a deathly, consumptive figure, and while she finds mometary happiness in the swirl of Christmas, Acts III and IV see the life force simply seeping out of her already racked, cadaverous figure. Musetta, on the other hand, is the life force incarnate, full of ebullience and action, including a skirt-lifting can-can during her famous waltz, and with temperament to burn. In the final scene, clad in warm orange-beige, she seems to be all goodness and tenderness as she becomes reconciled with Marcello.

Act III. In the snow outside the tavern, Mimi (Teresa Stratas) and Rodolfo (José Carreras) postpone their parting until the spring.

Set designs by Franco Zeffirelli for Act III (the tavern on the outskirts of Paris) and Act IV (the Parisian garret in early summer).

Opposite
Act IV. Rodolfo (José Carreras) reunited with the dying Mimi (Teresa Stratas).

Act IV. Colline (James Morris) bids farewell to the old overcoat he is about to sell—"Vecchia zimarra."

Opposite
Act IV. With the realization that Mimi is dead, Musetta (Renata Scotto) and Marcello (Richard Stilwell) are reconciled.

Each of the characters emerges with rich detail and individuality, as if Zeffirelli's work in films had brought increased clarity and focus to his stage work. His *Bohème* is full of tiny gestures that help to involve an audience with the action, and this "zoom lens" approach somehow reduces the feeling of set pieces and arias, so that the work flows from episode to episode in a drama operating on several levels at once. Reasons the director: "Singers used to think, 'We have to project, we have to be larger than life.' Nonsense! Callas demonstrated that the more realistic the acting, the stronger the bond with an audience. We don't need any hamming around, unless the character calls for it."

In the case of Colline, Zeffirelli worked with James Morris to be bigger than life and had him make large, sweeping gestures à la Chaliapin to define his personality. Marcello, on the other hand, is not an expounder but a listener. Using his eyes to absorb everything going on around him, he is drawn back to Musetta in Act II almost against his will, so strong is her magnetism. As Teresa Stratas noted, "Whoever he's directing, Franco will draw out facets of the personality which fit the

character. In my case, that means showing Mimi's vulnerability, a fragility coupled with outbursts of nervous energy. In an age of cynicism, Franco leads us by the hand saying, 'Look, life is beautiful, there's hope even in death.'"

The director-designer approaches all this with a kind of sensuousness, both visually and physically, that is at once realistic and human-scaled. For instance, he makes it clear that Mimi, as well as Rodolfo, is an experienced hand at love affairs; and neither one ever turns coy or cloying in their mutual attraction when they first meet. Each seems to welcome the lost key, the doused candle. Although Zeffirelli knows this is an almost foolproof opera to stage, one that works even in the most miserable of productions, he has aspired to elevate it to another plane. Having known *Bohème* since childhood—it was one of the first operas he ever saw, and he claims to have cried right through it—he is also aware of the unemotional and ironic depiction of struggling artists in Murger's novel.

While relishing Puccini's heart-on-sleeve romanticism, which never fails to deeply affect audiences, Zeffirelli senses that it is the grim poverty that gives the opera its bite: "This desperate group of youngsters, the misery and helplessness of being poor and young in Paris and having nothing but friendship and love—they're the only things that warm up your despair. And finally, despair takes over because it ends up in tragedy. That tragedy seals the memory of youth. From that moment on, youth is gone. In every city there are young people—artists, writers—who hope to succeed. Sometimes they starve. At that time there was hunger, people were dying. And it's a romantic horror and beauty of that kind of Paris that I think I hit rather sharply." The look of the opera had to be simple and early Romantic, focusing on the poor middle class painted by Gavarni and satirized by Daumier. Says Zeffirelli, "*La Bohème* is Puccini's marvelous song to poverty, happiness, and fantasy, a farewell to his youth as a starving conservatory student. He draws us into the lives of the same kids who eventually rebelled against the political and economic system."

Still, Zeffirelli remains more a doer and creator than a philosopher or conceptualizer, someone who, more than anything, seeks to engage and delight an audience, to take them out of themselves and away to another world. Of his artistic credo, he states simply, "I have no policy, no demagoguery, no ideals outside that of serving the audience and the authors and creating for myself a dream world, a world of fantasies that becomes real for the span of a performance. That's my ultimate purpose in life: to dream myself, enjoy myself, and help people to dream." And that's exactly what he has done with this dream *La Bohème*.

Boris Godunov

MUSSORGSKY

Production: **August Everding**   Sets: **Ming Cho Lee**
Costumes: **Peter J. Hall**

Boris Godunov

THERE WERE many significant aspects to the Met's boldly imaginative production of Mussorgsky's *Boris Godunov* in 1974. The work had originally been staged at the old house in 1913, and this was to be the first completely new production since that time, although numerous revivals had been mounted (in the 1952–53 edition, for example, the sets were repainted and—for scenes in need of refurbishing—scenery from an abandoned *Khovanshchina* and from *Un Ballo in maschera* was added). Then there was the question of the musical edition; the Met had previously played the standard Rimsky-Korsakov rescoring, as well as another version of Mussorgsky's original by Karol Rathaus. Now, for the first time, the theater returned to Mussorgsky's highly individual, rugged, original version, combining the best of his ideas from 1869 and 1872. Even allowing for the fact that a few cuts were made on this occasion, Met audiences were now offered more of *Boris Godunov* than any of their predecessors had heard in performance in the whole of the sixty years since the work's first staging there.

Returning to the Met to supervise this production was the German director August Everding, who had come to opera after a long association with legitimate theater, especially with Munich's city theater, the renowned Kammerspiele; there, he had been directing plays for nearly twenty years when—out of the blue in 1965—he received a call from Rudolf Hartmann, then head of the Bavarian State Opera, inviting him to mount a new production of *La Traviata*. The success of this

venture led to a commission from Vienna to direct *Tristan und Isolde* in 1968. It was also with that opera that he made his Met debut in 1971.

In preparing *Boris Godunov*, Everding was collaborating with the Chinese-American designer Ming Cho Lee, who, although making his Met debut, had already won a reputation with his work on Broadway and for the New York City Opera, including Ginastera's *Don Rodrigo* which had opened that company's first season at the New York State Theater in 1965. Together, they brought to this notoriously difficult, sprawling epic tale from Russian history a sense of cogency and unity, with the assistance of modern theatrical techniques. The massive sets were designed to enable changes to be made instantly, fluidly, between scenes; thus, one locale slid into the next with almost cinematic ease, thanks to the generous side stages, while Everding frequently favored the spotlit figure at the end of a scene so that the audience could focus on a personal emotional dilemma before the set for the next scene came into view. As with Mussorgsky's tragic national epic itself, Everding's style kept the observer alternating between the larger picture of Russian politics in the late sixteenth and early seventeenth century and the intense psychological panoply of personal ambitions, disappointments, confusions, and even tragedy, as in the case of the protagonist himself, that tortured, guilt-ridden, maddened czar of Russia. The textural alternation of massive and intimate, contrasting the public and the private, was underlined by the golden splendor of

Above

At the dress rehearsal, Martti Talvela as Boris is flanked by stage manager Chris Mahan and director August Everding; and (*right*) costume designs for Orthodox priests by Peter J. Hall.

◁ *Overleaf*

Act III, Scene 2. Boris (Martti Talvela), the guilt-ridden czar of Russia, now mortally stricken, reaches out to the surrounding boyars for support in the Great Hall of the Kremlin.

Lee's onion domes glowing in the background while bleak poverty consumed the Russian masses.

Everding reveals that this was the first and only time in his long career that he tackled *Boris Godunov*, even though he has directed Mussorgsky's *Khovanshchina* in Hamburg and was set to stage it for the Met during the 1985-86 season. "I did it because of my adoration for my friend Martti Talvela," he confesses. "I helped him found the festival at Savonlinna in Finland in 1973 with *Die Zauberflöte*. But two things in *Boris* interested me very much; the political relationship of Shouisky with the others, and then the human interest of the father and his relationship with his two children. Also the theology involved, because of my own early studies in that area and my knowledge of the Jesuits. I became fascinated by the rise and fall of Boris in terms of power, much like Shakespeare's *Richard II*—and what makes Boris crazy. Added to that was the European-Polish influence coming into this barbaric land."

Everding insists that the first thing that concerns him is "to tell the story, not to convert it to *my* story. The story is to be understood first, and I am suspicious if the public applauds at the rise of the curtain, because that means the designer has immediately told the whole story. Instead, it needs development. So designs should not be completely literal or realistic in telling a story of people onstage and their relationships. But in any work there is never just one way of doing it. A director must follow human beings and characters, take the personality of his actors and singers and use them onstage." With a designer such as Ming Cho Lee, Everding confers with him, explains the story as he sees it, and then tells him what he needs for his version, as well as stipulating the purely practical things, like a table or a step or whatever, that may be required. "The biggest change in music theater over the years," adds Everding, "is that it is not just singing, but an amalgamation of text and music and behavior and art and singing."

Overleaf ▷
Act I, Scene 2, The coronation outside St. Basil's Cathedral in Moscow, as the people call for Boris, their new czar; and (*right*) the newly crowned Boris (Martti Talvela), holding orb and scepter, attended by his son Feodor (Paul Offenkrantz).

Below
Act I, Scene 1. Outside a monastery near Moscow, peasants—goaded by guards—cry out to Boris to become the new czar.

This kind of amalgamation and completeness is evident as the curtain rises on his *Boris Godunov*. One immediately senses a strong, stark, brooding semirealism as being the key to both the direction and the design. Gone is the total pictorial realism that the Bolshoi Theater, for instance, maintains in re-creating late-sixteenth-century Russia, with its detailed scenic representation. Instead, this Met *Boris* conveys a spareness of directorial touch and design that seems to parallel Mussorgsky's own severe orchestration (now shorn of all the glittering accretions of the Rimsky-Korsakov edition). Sharply etched scenes combine to make up an epic tapestry in this primitive Russia, as delineated in Pushkin's chronicle play.

Everding strongly points up and magnifies the grasping for power which lies at the core of *Boris*. The czar himself, Grigori (the pretender Dimitri), Marina, Rangoni, Shouisky, the boyars—all these people are hungry for power, whether it be political or religious, or both. Everding's Moscow guards are presented as being cruel and violent toward the

unruly masses who hover in the darkness during the coronation. These fearful, angry, frustrated, downtrodden masses were made to be manipulated, and in this production they remain an anonymous crowd, not a collection of vignette characters. And yet, by extremely subtle means each one reveals aspects of a distinct personality in that choreographed collective. And as the actual, collective, hero of this opera, the Russian people swarm through its many scenes, from the opening one, in which they are coerced into calling for Boris as their next leader, through the powerful coronation scene and the St. Basil's and Kromy Forest episodes. At the same time, the leading character portrayals emerge as three-dimensional, strongly profiled people pitted against one another.

Everding brings many striking directorial touches to bear in making essential points. The desire for power and the domination of territories are manifested in the maps that clutter Boris's study, while Marina has at her fingertips in Poland a large world globe to spur her on to noble ambitions. The duality of the potent ruler and private family man is equally well conveyed. Even in the coronation scene, as the bells chime and the populace acclaim their new ruler, one feels that the gold-encrusted Boris is isolated from the real world around him as, in his jeweled robes, he stands spotlit in relief—a man set apart from the faceless masses who have helped to put him on the throne.

With Martti Talvela in the title role, Everding conceived this czar as a tortured, barbaric figure of brute force, a towering giant, menacing, cruel, and dominant even in the tragic downfall—but also a man capable of great tenderness. Playing on

Talvela's larger-than-life stature, Everding contrives—by means of controlled, even restrained, direction—to give this portrayal of Boris a sense of grandeur with concentration, command, and honesty, eschewing hammy effects. This proves especially true in the clock scene of Act II, as Boris cringes in his hallucinations under a heavy, toppled study table, having just clawed down the drapes of his study entrance with compelling fierceness; and again in Act III, in his extraordinarily theatrical death scene on the crimson steps of the Great Hall of the Kremlin—a scene containing a wealth of vocal dynamics and inflection. This heroic portrayal ends with a full-body fall down those steps, like a felled tree, ending spread-eagled in a breathtaking dramatic climax.

Especially effective, too, is the presentation of Boris's son Feodor, weeping (and with good reason) as he assumes the throne while his father lies lifeless and the dark, hooded monks prostrate themselves before their new ruler; small and frightened, he seems lost in the vast spaces of his father's gilded throne. Down the centuries, Russia has witnessed, among its succession of rulers, mysterious deaths and constant grabbing for power, and Everding's staging evokes this historic

thread to chilling effect: indeed, in Scene 1 of the final act, we are made to feel this at St. Basil's, as Boris stares directly at his accuser when, with idiot sincerity, the Simpleton scorns the ruler for seizing power by murder.

Lee's settings, the results of a summer spent in Moscow studying Russian architecture, appear to be based on the theme of an iconostasis, the sanctuary screen of gold-and-red icons that stands before the altar of an Orthodox Church. The haunting, haunted faces of saints and angels gaze down with sadness on this enactment of history below, emitting the feeling of religion as a stringent and even mysterious force in the drama. The crudity of Russia in the era portrayed is suggested in the coronation scene by the raw-timbered bell towers erected on either side of the magnificent St. Basil's, whose architectural form and details are conveyed in terms of strongly etched elements rather than of architectural completeness. The towers themselves were designed to look as if they had been hastily constructed for the occasion, and the very grimness of the set, as contrasted with the festive nature of the music and the joy that the populace is expected to feel, make for a scene rich in psychological depth.

Act II, Scene 1. Bored with life, the Polish princess Marina (Mignon Dunn), with her ladies in her apartments, ponders future glory.

Above

Act II, Scene 1. Marina (Mignon Dunn) and the scheming monk Rangoni (William Dooley), who advises the vain Polish princess how best to further her political ambitions.

Left

Act III. The ceremonial entry, in the Kromy Forest scene, of the pretender Dimitri (Harry Theyard); behind the soldiers bearing the platform are the Jesuits Chernikovsky (Charles Anthony) and Lavitsky (Robert Goodloe).

Above
Act III, Scene 1. Boris (Martti Talvela) is accosted by peasants outside St. Basil's Cathedral.

But many images linger in the mind: the bleak, rugged stone walls of the Novodievichy Monastery, and those outside St. Basil's Cathedral, with the familiar gold onion domes glowing mystically in the distance; the colorful details of Boris's study with its tapestries and icons; the soft blue-and-white luxury of Marina's rooms and the moonlit Sandomir garden with its graceful marble Renaissance staircase and three flowing fountains, together with the strangely stylized trees in almost cubist fashion; the red magnificence of the icon-filled Great Hall in the Kremlin, with its funereal candelabra and golden throne. Perhaps only in the final Kromy Forest scene (placed last, where it belongs, for it is here through the Simpleton's words that we sense the eternal sadness of Russia and its besieged people, the death of Boris and the coming of the pretender Dimitri being just another episode in a long, brutal history) does Everding fail to do the drama full justice. His revolutionary mobs never become demonic enough, and Dimitri's entrance, not on horseback, but borne in—*à la* Radames in the triumphal scene in *Aida*—on a shoulder-held platform, lacks some of its potential dramatic impact. But overall—with Peter J. Hall's exquisite costumes, contrasting the bleakness of the peasants' garb with opulent fur-trimmed velvet robes for Boris, with a charming polonaise created by George Balanchine for the Polish episode in Act II, and with the expert use of the Met's stage machinery—Everding's ten scenes flow smoothly, quickly, dramatically, with remarkable cumulative momentum, telling the story, made up of many disparate elements, with clearheaded focus, honesty, and theatrical strength.

Left and above
In Act I the Simpleton (Andrea Velis) bemoans the fate of Holy Russia; and the scene in the Great Hall of the Kremlin in Act III, with the dying Boris (Martti Talvela) and his son Feodor (Paul Offenkrantz) seated on the throne he will inherit.

Cavalleria Rusticana

MASCAGNI

Pagliacci

LEONCAVALLO

Production: **Franco Zeffirelli**
Sets and Costumes: **Franco Zeffirelli**

Cavalleria Rusticana and Pagliacci

A PARCHED village square situated high in the desolate Sicilian mountains, and an equally barren, rocky, open spot on the coast of Calabria in Southern Italy—these were the locales that Franco Zeffirelli, with his keen eye for physical and human detail, sought to re-create at the Metropolitan Opera House in January 1970. In so doing, he captured onstage the full flavor of the places, the people, the veristic passions and personal heartbreak that complement one another so powerfully in Mascagni's *Cavalleria rusticana* and Leoncavallo's *Pagliacci*. These two works—traditionally paired and both having originated in the last decade of the nineteenth century, in 1890 and 1892 respectively—have become the very epitome of *verismo* in Italian opera. *Verismo* may be defined as theatrical realism, which demands more than large-scale emotions and hysterical breast-beating. It calls for minute attention to be focused on those specific details that tell us how people live, love, and die. *Verismo*, after all, was inspired by the realistic novels of Emile Zola in 1870s France, and one could even say that *verismo* in Italian opera took its cue from Bizet's Mérimée-inspired *Carmen* of 1875, whose brutality and harsh realism shocked the Paris bourgeoisie when it was first performed. In the Italian repertory, Verdi's treatment of a real-life demimondaine in *La Traviata* (itself deriving from a French play) was a kind of precursor of what Mascagni, Leoncavallo, Cilèa, Giordano, and others were to fashion from the lives of real people toward the end of the nineteenth century. It is interesting that these composers often turned for their stories to the most exciting new stage plays and novels or to contemporary events.

The reason why Zeffirelli's tremendously absorbing, full-blooded *Cav* and *Pag* make such a strong emotional impact is that he has looked beyond the principal characters that populate these domestic tragedies, by making their worlds, their existences, spring vividly to life, and by giving them a completely realistic ambience in which their passions can be ignited. Giovanni Verga, the author of the short story that inspired Mascagni, had turned it into a play as a vehicle for the seductive talents of Eleonora Duse, and it was in paying homage to that fabled Italian actress that Zeffirelli chose to stage *Cavalleria rusticana* in the way he did. His Santuzza represents what he imagines the legendary Duse must have been like in that role. The story had its roots in the Sicilian village in which Verga grew up. When visiting such hill-towns not far from Catania or Siracusa, one instantly becomes aware of the hot, dry, oppressive atmosphere, in which jealousies, illicit love affairs, and violence lurk just below the well-ordered surface, ready to explode at any moment. In these villages one sees women forever swathed in black from head to foot, mourning husbands, sons, family, with a fierce passion and commitment that seem to derive their tragic character from the black, lava-based soil that typifies eastern Sicily. The Church and its religious festivals bring whatever color, glamour, theater, and wonder these people ever experience in a land where life and death are primary matters, where hard physical work and scraping a bare existence are the norm.

Such is the world that Zeffirelli skillfully brings to life with his single set, revealed at once as Mascagni's sweeping score begins. Even before Turiddu's distant serenade to Lola is heard echoing through the empty, still-dark square, the somber, black-clad figure of the sleepless, suicidal Santuzza is seen. Just as the stars begin to fade in the predawn sky, she hurtles through the square and up the massive, steep steps leading to the equally massive stone church which dominates the town and serves as the magnetic focus for everyone living in the vicinity. Zeffirelli immediately establishes the fatal triangle that will culminate in violence and death on this Easter morning: Santuzza has been excommunicated because of her illicit relationship with Turiddu and resulting pregnancy; and it is Turiddu's confident voice that is heard singing to the carter's wife, Lola. Zeffirelli, the designer, artfully conveys the hilltop locale of the village, with its red-tiled roofs and sun-bleached stone houses clinging to the hillsides, huddled together in the shadow of the church. With the dawning of a new day, the village comes to life: people emerge from their houses, shutters are thrown open on wrought-iron balconies, rugs are beaten, and shops (including the hardened,

Above

During a rehearsal of *Cavalleria rusticana*, Grace Bumbry (as Santuzza) receives guidance from director Franco Zeffirelli.

◁ *Overleaf*

Cavalleria rusticana: The Easter Day procession in the village square, with Santuzza (Grace Bumbry) and Lucia (Carlotta Ordassy) kneeling by the table in the left foreground.

inured Mamma Lucia's wine shop) open their doors for business. Preparations are being made for Easter Mass, the church being festooned in wine-red swags for this meaningful day in the Christian calendar. But somberness prevails, for the morning light is shot through with gray; when the villagers change from everyday work clothes and don their Sunday best, these are mainly black, brown, gray, dark in tone.

Into this scene comes the popular and successful carter, Alfio, in his brightly colored horse-drawn cart with its traditional Sicilian folk paintings in vibrant shades of red, yellow, and blue. Alfio, obviously the town's *nouveau riche*, looks dashing in his holiday finery, but even more striking, when she later turns up for church, is his sultry young wife's holiday dress—a hot-pink and orange creation with gold embroidery.

The scene is thus set for the impressive Easter Day procession, and here Zeffirelli spares nothing in order to encapsulate the splendor, pageantry, and sheer theatricality of the occasion. He superbly catches the pomp and ostentation of the church, contrasted with the simple lives of the local populace. The slow parade of church officials, choirboys, mysteriously masked figures, police, and others—one can even sense the strenuous effort of their climb up the jagged hill—has as its climax the golden figure of the Madonna borne aloft with candles and glitter, creating for the villagers that culminating sense of awe and wonder and devotion.

Cavalleria rusticana. Alfio (Frank Guarrera), by his colorfully painted cart, boasts of his travels and his attractive wife Lola.

After the church service, Turiddu (Franco Corelli)—in a brindisi—exhorts the worshippers to drink—"Viva il vino spumaggiante."

Opposite
Betrayed by Turiddu, Santuzza (Grace Bumbry) tells his mother, Lucia (Carlotta Ordassy), that he has become the lover of another man's wife.

Although Santuzza is seen praying along with the villagers, there is an underlying feeling of the tension created between, on the one hand, the magnetic force that is the Church, and, on the other, the girl's being barred from its ministrations. Then she pours out her torment to the compassionate though resigned, life-weary Mamma Lucia, but is left alone on the broad stone steps when Mass begins inside. She waits—as if stalking her prey—for Turiddu, who arrives late. For him their affair is over, and he tries to push past this possessed woman, to brush her off, failing to understand even a little the intensity of her feelings for him, or how much their relationship has meant to her, and the damage he has done to her standing in this tightly knit community. With the arrival of Lola, the triangle becomes visually and dramatically complete: the young, sexy, richly turned-out girl set against the more matronly, salt-of-the-earth creature, while Turiddu is seen to be merely a Sicilian cad, confidently brushing one affair aside for the next, running a comb through his hair, preening, cocky in his evident sexuality.

Once Lola has disappeared into the church, the passionate confrontation begins. Santuzza blocks Turiddu's path and a violent emotional exchange takes place on the deserted steps, leading to Turiddu's throwing Santuzza to the ground. Losing his temper, he throws her down again, and—brought to the brink—Santuzza now hurls her curse, "A te la mala Pasqua," before collapsing and rolling down the steps, her body drained in defeat. But Santuzza will be avenged, and she tells Alfio what he has suspected all along. He too enters the church, leaving the desperate, hysterical Santuzza to calm herself at the water fountain in the deserted square.

As the women walk home to prepare Easter dinner, the men gather for a glass of wine, and amid toasts and camaraderie, Alfio challenges Turiddu to a duel, biting his ear in time-honored fashion. Still cocky, but frightened too, Turiddu bids "Addio" to his mother—she seems casual at first, knowing his penchant for melodrama, but eventually becomes aware of his impending fate—and runs to confront Alfio, the men silently taking sides. At the close, the sky grows stormier, more threatening, and a woman's voice is heard pronouncing "Hanno ammazzato compare Turiddu!" before the scorned Santuzza once again hurtles into the maelstrom of this village square, avenged but grief-stricken at the tragic outcome.

Santuzza (Grace Bumbry) pleads with the reluctant Turiddu (Franco Corelli) to remember their love.

Surface appearances versus unbridled passions roiling just underneath are equally well captured by Zeffirelli in his handling of *Pagliacci*. In the forlorn setting of Montalto, the arrival of the traveling players is, along with Easter and Christmas, one of the events that bring joy into the drab lives of the hard-working inhabitants. Tonio delivers his Prologue against a background of multicolored spotlights on the gold curtain. For this Sherrill Milnes was dressed in clown's costume (looking forward to the play within a play of Act II), but he could never agree with Zeffirelli about this, feeling that the actor-singer who plays Tonio should recite the Prologue as himself "because the facial features are frozen in the white makeup and wig, and you can't convey the serious 'we are real people and we also bleed' feeling. But it's always an experience to work with Franco—even though he kept procrastinating about the duet with Nedda in Act I. The fact is, Teresa Stratas and I staged it

with bits and pieces. Then we showed it to Franco, and he loved it. I got clobbered with the whip and rolled down the ramp, but I'm not afraid to do it— as long as I put baseball guards on my elbows."

In Act I the players are welcomed by the townspeople in their buttoned-up Sunday best, the children treated to colorful balloons. Into this rocky terrain come the "Grande Compagnia" of *i pagliacci* in their horse-drawn covered cart, which Zeffirelli ingeniously uses not only for the players' travel and to drum up business for the night's performance, but later also as part of their modest show—Beppe sings his serenade from it at some distance from the main stage. A great gnarled tree stands alone on the promontory against the dramatic hot-orange, cloud-swirled skyscape, a sunset that changes to deeper and deeper shades of russet and violet as night falls and the internal drama reaches its explosion. Canio arrives in full clown's costume, he and his troupe having promised the

Above

Pagliacci, Act I. The arrival of the strolling players, with Sherrill Milnes as Tonio (left), Richard Tucker as Canio in clown's costume, and Teresa Stratas as Nedda.

Overleaf ▷

Pagliacci, Act I. The strolling players' wagon at rest outside Montalto, Calabria; Nedda (Teresa Stratas), caressing a child member of the troupe, gazes upward, envying the freedom of the birds.

public a grand entertainment that evening. But while he warns one villager against joking about marital infidelity, he changes his clothes and becomes a cigar-smoking, small-time entrepreneur in a loud checked suit, dashing off to the village on business, leaving Nedda and Tonio behind to prepare for the show.

Part of Zeffirelli's genius lies in his method of creating a place and a purpose for these trapped, frustrated characters. This traveling band includes a fire-eater and three acrobat children, on whom Nedda lavishes her affections, for she and Canio have no children of their own. As a fire is being built and supper prepared, she dreams about the freedom of the birds she sees overhead, creating a warm sense of improvised familial intimacy. But the true state of things in Nedda's everyday world is brought into focus with a vengeance when Tonio begins to press his attentions on her, and she—cornered in a highly compromising situation—grabs the whip, then the knife, with which she half-blinds the man. Like a maimed animal, he tumbles down the rocky incline. Seeking revenge, he returns with Canio to prove to him the fact of Nedda's blatant infidelity with Silvio, and Canio—his rage somewhat subdued by Beppe, who reminds him of the performance to be given—is left alone, against a darkening sky and a leafless tree, for the exposure of his soul in "Vesti la giubba." He is a simple, lonely, aging man shattered by the failure in his real life, and forced to play the clown onstage.

Below and opposite
Pagliacci, Act I. After Nedda has been caught with her lover Silvio, Tonio (Sherrill Milnes) tells her husband Canio (Richard Tucker) to wait before taking vengeance; and Canio (James McCracken) puts on the makeup of a clown, even though his heart is breaking—"Vesti la giubba."

Pagliacci, Act II. Nedda
(Teresa Stratas) costumed as
Colombina in the players'
evening show, in which
Taddeo the clown (*inset*) is
performed by Tonio (Sherrill
Milnes).

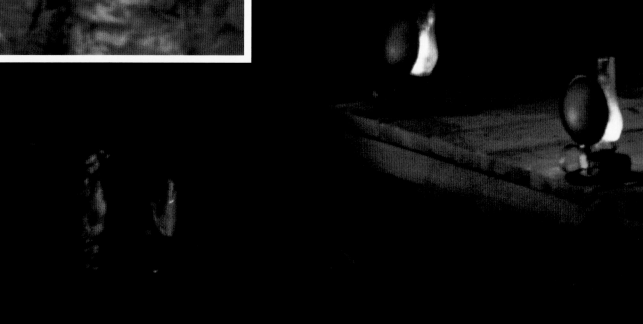

Under a brilliant cobalt sky the actors play to their customers, seated on benches facing the impromptu red-and-blue stage with festive lamps hung above it. Zeffirelli's clever table for Colombina, which rises from and sinks into the floor, along with the gaudy ragtag commedia dell'arte of the show, provides a sharp comic contrast to the personal drama that finally erupts into the open as art and life become one onstage. With Canio no longer able to conceal his jealous rage over his fickle wife—both onstage in the play and in real life—he maniacally stabs first her, then Silvio, wildly dragging her into the midst of the horrified crowd for the final plunge of the knife and the pronouncement "La commedia è finita." The veristic brutality and horrible finality of this delirious, violent act leave both the onstage spectators and the theater audience stunned.

Leoncavallo had read about such a case in his local newspaper, and the story inspired him to write *Pagliacci*. In viewing Zeffirelli's tight, taut, three-dimensional staging, one can almost feel that the opera represents real-life drama, not some stagey piece of artifice. The line of communication between public and stage is immediate, direct, unobstructed, electric, for here is a northern Italian director who can convey the reality of such southern Italian brutality, in a world of betrayal, heartbreak, and volcanic eruptions, with masterly conviction.

Above and right
Pagliacci, Act II. The entrance of Pagliaccio, played by Canio (Richard Tucker), in the play within a play; and the clown stands over the body of his beloved Nedda (Atsuka Azuma), whom he has murdered.

Director Franco Zeffirelli (center, right) onstage during an
early rehearsal for Act I of *Pagliacci*.

Les Contes d'Hoffmann

OFFENBACH

Production: **Otto Schenk**   Sets: **Günther Schneider-Siemssen**
Costumes: **Gaby Frey**   Lighting: **Gil Wechsler**

Les Contes d'Hoffmann

THE phantasmagorical world of *Les Contes d'Hoffmann* is one of macabre visions, of romantic imagination, of evil forces, of mysterious, magical events far beyond ordinary human experience. This can be interpreted in a great variety of ways, from the symbolic and abstract to the fervent realism sought in the early nineteenth century by the writer E. T. A. Hoffmann himself or later in the century by Offenbach and his librettists, Georges Barbier and Michel Carré. It was this latter and inspired realism that the ever-inventive director Otto Schenk and his designer, Günther Schneider-Siemssen, adopted at the Met in March 1982 and which was apparent from the first, characterful, view of Luther's subterranean Nuremberg tavern to the final tableau of the Epilogue, in which the poet Hoffmann, alone in the deserted tavern, scribbles his wild, febrile tales on the poster announcing that night's opera, *Don Giovanni*, which he has impetuously torn from the wall in a fit of creative release.

Schenk and Schneider-Siemssen, together with the costume designer Gaby Frey, waved a magic wand over *Les Contes d'Hoffmann*, imbuing it with rich visual fantasy and theatrical allure, as well as a strong Hoffmannesque undertone of grotesquerie, even diablerie. This was a lively, entertaining, often gripping *Hoffmann*, which would resonate in the audience's imagination for a long time afterward, for it struck at the very heart of the work and its broad canvas of characters with rare honesty and without superfluous gimmicks or "interpretation." As a result, it emerged as a compelling narrative tale that fully involved its public. The only puzzling decision was a musical one, since the Met stayed with the standard Choudens edition,

ignoring the important research of the past few years that has resulted in the *Urtext*, as published in the Oeser edition; the latter attempts to assemble everything that Offenbach had intended for the completion of the *Hoffmann* he had long envisioned in his own mind, but which was prevented by his death in 1881. What the composer sought to convey in this, his single serious opera in a life's work otherwise filled with diverting *opéras bouffes*, may never be totally clear, given that the sketches were assembled only after his death. Still, a reasonable approximation of his intentions now exists and had been staged—two seasons previously—by the Greater Opera of Miami in a production also designed by Schneider-Siemssen, whose Met version bears a close resemblance to what he had created for Miami.

By playing the drama straight, Schenk avoids any search for profound symbolism. He does not seem concerned whether Hoffmann's four loves actually involve the same unattainable woman (in this production each part was taken by a different soprano; in a later season Catherine Malfitano did in fact play the quartet of the poet's loves), or whether his friend Nicklausse is an alter ego or the muse of poetry, or whether his four nemeses are incarnations of the Devil, hallucinations, the product of extreme paranoia or of the poet's own destructive tendencies. It is possible to look at Hoffmann's bizarre tales and the Barbier-Carré adaptation of them in any number of lights, all of them fascinating and provocative. But Schenk, in keeping with his typical straightforward, no-nonsense style, has chosen to take the direct approach, stressing the humanity and pathos of Hoffmann and his ill-starred adventures.

Born in Vienna, Schenk began his theatrical career as an actor, studying at the famous Reinhardt Seminar. When he began acting, he always tried to teach his colleagues how to act as well; slowly but surely he was pushed into being a director by his fellow actors. Eventually, after performing at Vienna's Volkstheater and in cellar theater (Vienna's equivalent of off-Broadway), he made his home at the Josefstadt Theater, where he still occasionally acts and directs. Schenk's first assignment in opera came in 1961 when the Vienna Volksoper asked him to stage Donizetti's *Don Pasquale*; and the next year he directed Berg's *Lulu* at the Theater an der Wien for the Vienna Festival Weeks. Einem's *Dantons Tod*, Janáček's *Jenůfa* and Strauss's *Der Rosenkavalier* followed, as did a staging of *Die Zauberflöte* in 1964 at Salzburg. In 1965 the Vienna State Opera named him chief stage director, and today he acts as a consultant there while fulfilling directing engagements all over the world. His *Die Fledermaus* (for Vienna and Munich) and a highly praised *Contes d'Hoffmann* (for the Volksoper, with Anja Silja in all four roles as Hoffmann's loves) have become trademarks of his extremely personal approach to opera work.

Schenk first came to the Metropolitan for a new *Tosca* in 1968 at the suggestion of soprano Birgit Nilsson, who had strongly recommended him to Rudolf Bing. His approach remains simple and to the point. Of operatic works he has said: "You can find ways to show their relevance. You can also do them as period pieces, as antique operas—why not? Our rooms are often filled with antiques, old things we love, that tell us about the past. We can treat operas either way." Schenk chose to let Hoffmann's three tales unravel naturally and realistically, so that the macabre elements stand out in bold relief against the somber, naturalistic backgrounds. Schenk and Schneider-Siemssen seemed to have a single purpose, for the designer envisioned highly detailed, realistic-cum-fantastic visions of the eccentric inventor-physicist Spalanzani's workship, Giulietta's languorous, menacing Venetian courtyard, and Crespel's bourgeois Munich home, the three scenes framed by the claustrophobic, overheated beery atmosphere of Luther's crowded tavern of the Prologue and Epilogue. Frey's costumes too were rich in period detail, with all four heroines in pure white, and each of the nemeses in harsh black to provide a thematic thread that runs throughout the course of each story of Hoffmann's disastrous loves.

Right
Act I. Coppélius (James Morris) with some examples of Spalanzani's inventions.

Act I. The fantastic house of the mad inventor Spalanzani (Andrea Velis), who lies prostrate following the destruction of his creation, Olympia, while his rival Coppélius (Michael Devlin) exults and Nicklausse (Anne Howells), Hoffmann (Placido Domingo), and Andrès (Michel Sénéchal) look on.

Most breathtaking is the team's Act I, as Luther's dark, cozy cellar tavern (evoking the labyrinthine terrors of Hoffmann's frequent drinking bouts) is made to disappear slowly, as it sinks into the ground, thanks to the Met's efficient elevator system, and the mad scientist Spalanzani's cheery but nutty workshop sails forward as if out of the dark, swirling shadows of the mind—a virtual treasure trove of whirring mechanical devices, toys, flying half-human creatures, and wheels, large and small. These gaily spinning contraptions, some—disconcertingly—seeming to have a life all their own, exemplify the nineteenth century's fixation with trying to imbue inanimate objects with living qualities. One's eyes search this fantastic room, with all its moving parts, its magical mechanical contraptions, its fun-house fantasy, its glowing beakers, and Olympia is found to be housed in a mysterious box to stage left, its opening door emitting an eerie diagonal shaft of light before she appears. This magnificent mechanical doll has been endowed with remarkable human attributes, qualities that make her all the more

threatening and unpredictable to everyone around her, especially Cochenille, with whom she indulges in a sequence of witty and brilliantly timed by-play. This willful, wind-up Olympia employs a seemingly detachable jaw and fingers that need twisting to enable her to accomplish her coloratura feats; she is capable of producing superhuman echo effects while bent in half at the waist, as well as evincing delectable panic when singing the fearsome cadenzas of her showpiece song. Yet even as a fantastic creature, the product of man, she is made to appear almost manic in her concentration and her reeling movement—a robot figure about to go berserk.

Schenk's guests for this miraculous, curious event, have the air of a group exploring one of the French capital's nineteenth-century Expositions Universelles, an unsavory bunch of bourgeois decadents with no human feeling whatsoever and none of them fooled for a moment by this life-size doll, yet completely intrigued. The eager, boyish Hoffmann offers the only real show of emotions in this crowd, and when, as the butt of a joke and to everyone else's merriment, the mechanical object of Hoffmann's blind affection is torn apart by the raging Dr. Coppélius before his very eyes, the effect is truly horrifying—and for Hoffmann truly heartbreaking. His vision of the ideal woman, of ideal love, is literally shattered before his eyes.

An oozing sensuality characterizes the darkly dangerous, mysterious, rotting Venice, the world of the courtesan Giulietta. Schneider-Siemssen provides her with an open courtyard, a view of the gondola-dotted canals with projections of the neighboring palazzos, and a warmly lit residence on the left. Into this shadowy, depraved, moonlit atmosphere enters the black-clad Dappertutto, proffering his glittering diamond to the avaricious woman if she will wrest Hoffmann's shadow from the lustful, passionate man. Schenk's direction remains surprisingly static in this act, but Giulietta's cold, calculating nature makes her the flame to which such a moth as Hoffmann is drawn—and with disastrous results, for, although he thinks he will possess her, the heartless creature cruelly escapes with Pitichinaccio.

Opposite and left
Act II. Hoffmann's second nemesis, Dappertutto (Michael Devlin), whose sword the poet uses in his duel with Schlémil; and Günther Schneider-Siemssen's model set for the palazzo on the Grand Canal in Venice.

Overleaf ▷
Act II. (*Right*) The cold-hearted Venetian courtesan Giulietta (Tatiana Troyanos) with one of her many admirers, Pitichinaccio (Michel Sénéchal).
Act III. (*Left*) Hoffmann (Alfredo Kraus) with his third love, the young singer Antonia (Catherine Malfitano); and the sinister Dr. Miracle (Michael Devlin), who claims he can cure Antonia.

Les Contes d'Hoffmann 63

Act III. Dr. Miracle (Michael Devlin) confronts Antonia's father, Crespel (John Macurdy), in his living room; and (*below*) the deaf servant Frantz (Michel Sénéchal) sings his couplets by Antonia's spinet.

Antonia's drawing room in Munich possesses a lovely homey quality with its heavily draped windows, piano, and fireplace, above which hangs the portrait of the consumptive girl's celebrated mother—an opera singer who died at the hands of the sinister, cadaverous Dr. Miracle. Cleverly, these seemingly solid protective walls are rendered transparent when Miracle is left alone with his vulnerable patient, and through these walls the pathetic Antonia can dream of glory in the opera house, while nightmarish effects erupt in every corner as the terrifying Miracle vanishes and reappears magically through the floor, in the grandfather's clock, and in an explosion of fire in the fireplace, brandishing his vials and violin. The overall effect is similar to that produced by a spooky horror film in the tradition of *Dr. Caligari*. As Antonia sings and sings at the command of her mother's voice (conjured up by Miracle), she expires from her exertions, left limp in the arms of the ever-compassionate, love-struck Hoffmann.

Munich recedes from view, only to return the audience to Luther's tavern, filled with drunken students who have held onto Hoffmann's every word. The poet, now drunk beyond hearing and comprehension, suffers his final degradation as the singer Stella, who has been performing in *Don Giovanni* that night, arrives for her rendezvous with Hoffmann, only to be swept off on the arm of the councilor Lindorf. Urged on by his Muse (Nicklausse transformed), Hoffmann is left with only his art, fed by the experiences of his own tragic love life. Beginning as a raving alcoholic, and resembling a crazed, disheveled, unshaven, romantic—bellicose in temperament, and bespectacled in the line of Schubert or Schumann—this haunted genius of a Hoffmann finds himself, by the end, deserted, alone with his Muse, as a solo violin intones his poignant melody in the background. The plight of this flailing, spent, febrile poet, his soul literally laid bare before our eyes, is made deeply moving in Schenk's presentation of this series of intense and ever more destructive love affairs. With Placido Domingo as Hoffmann, Schenk had a singer-actor of tremendous dramatic gifts, and this is a role to which Domingo responds with splendid nuance, intensity, and commitment. Schenk, like a master surgeon, helped the tenor to achieve a remarkable baring of the human soul onstage. As one critic noted, this production of *Les Contes d'Hoffmann* appeared to be "a restoration of some kind of primal sense of theater as make-believe." It was make-believe that made one believe.

Opposite
Act III. The ill-fated girl (Catherine Malfitano), tormented by desire to be a singer like her mother.

Falstaff

VERDI

Production: **Franco Zeffirelli**
Sets and Costumes: **Franco Zeffirelli**

Falstaff

ONE could say that Franco Zeffirelli came to Verdi's *Falstaff* naturally, almost as a matter of course. His mother's cousin is Ines Alfani-Tellini, who had played Nannetta in Arturo Toscanini's historic *Falstaff* at La Scala in the 1920s. After her retirement from the stage she held master classes at Siena's Accademia Chigiana, and there she let the young Zeffirelli supervise year-end stagings of operas with her students. Zeffirelli, first with experience as an actor, than as a designer (following studies in architecture in his native Florence), came to opera with a comic work when in 1954 he directed Rossini's *La Cenerentola* at La Scala, for which production of course he was also the designer; earlier, he had gained notice for his designs for Shakespeare's *Troilus and Cressida* in the Boboli Gardens.

It was with *Falstaff* that Zeffirelli made his debut at the Metropolitan Opera in 1964, a year marking the 400th anniversary of Shakespeare's birth, as well as the first performance of this work—Verdi's only comic opera—at the Met since the 1948-49 season, when the work itself did not find popular favor. Now, however, Zeffirelli provided the theater with one of the most spectacular, lavish, and enchanting productions in its history—giving the work new popular appeal. Over the years the director-designer has turned his attention to this masterpiece of Verdi's final years no fewer than seven times, including productions at Covent Garden and the Holland Festival before his Met debut. Zeffirelli has said that the two operatic works that continue to fascinate him the most are

Mozart's *Don Giovanni* and Verdi's *Falstaff*, because of their central characters. "Despite all his disillusionment," he observes, "Falstaff is always ready to believe again, to start again. Each time he falls into the trap laid for him, but he never really gets very angry. An extraordinary character!"

When the curtains first parted on this *Falstaff*, an evening on which Leonard Bernstein made his Met debut as well, what the audience glimpsed was a remarkably realistic, yet idealized Elizabethan Windsor, complete with half-timbered Tudor houses, rough balustraded balconies and glowing leaded-glass windows, and a magical Windsor Forest spreading around a gnarled, towering Herne's Oak. In essence, Zeffirelli created a Merrie England with an Italianate warmth. As he has noted of his mentor, the brilliant Luchino Visconti (who hired the then young aspiring actor in 1947 and eventually made him his assistant and let him design his productions), he "taught me that everything in a production is of equal importance, right down to the tiniest detail." That exceptional sense of period detail and character delineation was to mark Zeffirelli's *Falstaff* as he took his audience into a make-believe world of Shakespeare via Boito, the poet who gave shape and concision to the material—distilled from *The Merry Wives of Windsor* as well as *Henry IV*, Parts I and II—in his glorious libretto.

Above

Conductor Leonard Bernstein discusses musical points with Judith Raskin, who sang Nannetta in the original production in 1964, and Gabriella Tucci, the first Alice.

◁ *Overleaf*

Act I, Scene 1. The fat knight Falstaff (Geraint Evans) wrily questions the meaning of honor—"L'Onore."
(*Right*) Design by Franco Zeffirelli for the Garter Inn.

Opposite and above

Act I, Scene 2. In the garden of Ford's house, the Merry Wives discover that both Alice and Meg have received identical love letters from Falstaff: Alice (Gabriella Tucci), at the top of the steps, with her daughter Nannetta (Judith Raskin) below her, and Meg (Mildred Miller) with Quickly (Regina Resnik). As the plot thickens, Fenton (Luigi Alva) steals a kiss from his sweetheart Nannetta (Jeannette Pilou).

Act I, Scene 2. The garden of Ford's house in Windsor, with Dr. Cajus (Paul Franke), Ford (Kostas Paskalis), Fenton (Luigi Alva), Bardolfo (Andrea Velis), and Pistola (Norman Scott).

Act II, Scene 2. Zeffirelli's design for the interior of Ford's house (*above*). Inside the house (*below*), Falstaff (Anselmo Colzani) is hurried into hiding by Alice Ford (Gabriella Tucci) and Quickly (Regina Resnik), and moments later he is secreted in a laundry basket (*right*), attended by Meg (Rosalind Elias) and Quickly, as Ford (Mario Sereni, holding sword) returns after searching adjacent rooms; meanwhile, Fenton (Luigi Alva) and Nannetta (Judith Raskin) are engrossed in their own private world.

Zeffirelli's production proved a breakthrough for the Rudolf Bing regime at the Met. The general manager had favored simpler painted settings in the numerous new productions since his takeover in 1950, but this probably had to do with the limited stage and storage facilities that were available before the move from the old house. In welcoming this new production style, the critics outdid themselves with superlatives. Writing in the *Herald Tribune*, Alan Rich called it "more than a brilliant achievement. It is a milestone in the history of operatic production in this city, a gigantic forward step in the conception of opera,

and a challenge that will be met only with the utmost difficulty." Rich went on to write that Zeffirelli had realized Richard Wagner's dream of opera as *Gesamtkunstwerk*, a total work of art— that cohesive unity of words, music, and visual effects. Every nuance and detail of this long-misunderstood work came to life visually, with Zeffirelli orchestrating the stage as though the composer himself had worked with colors and movements, rather than with notes. Everything emerged out of the music itself. If in Act I, Scene 2, the music seems full of butterflies, then onstage Nannetta and Fenton are seen chasing one another through banks of tall flowers like the infatuated, preoccupied teenagers they really are. When Falstaff goes off at his appointed hour to woo Mistress Ford at her house and the music seems to evoke the idea of garlands, Zeffirelli has the fat knight wearing these same garlands in his effort to be as youthfully romantic as possible. And in the Act III forest scene there is a brilliant spark of light just as Nannetta echoes a heaven-borne phrase in Fenton's aria, and the director has the girl herself pop out from behind a tree wearing a gossamer elfin headdress that seems to spring out of the enchanted music itself.

Left
Act II, Scene 2. Alice Ford
(Renata Tebaldi), bemused
but uncertain as she is courted
by Falstaff.

Act II, Scene 1. At the Garter
Inn (*right*), the jealous Ford
(Kostas Paskalis) curses the
prospect of being cuckolded—
"E sogno? o realtà?" Earlier,
Dame Quickly (Regina
Resnik) has paid her respects
to Falstaff (Geraint Evans) as a
time is set for his rendezvous
with Ford's wife, Alice.

Act III, Scene 2. In Windsor Forest the principals join in the final fugue—"Tutto nel mondo è burla." From left to right are: Alice (Renata Tebaldi), Quickly (Regina Resnik), Fenton (Luigi Alva), Bardolfo (Andrea Velis), Falstaff (Geraint Evans), Pistola (Richard Best), Nannetta (Jeannette Pilou), Meg (Joann Grillo), and Cajus (Paul Franke).

This sense of musical and visual unity dominates from the very first scene, set in the rough-and-ready Garter Inn, until the final fugue sung by the entire cast, which declares that everything in the world is but a jest. Rough beams, heavy dishes, pewter jugs, ropes, clutter, and a giant wine cask dominate the Garter Inn, as well it might in Falstaff's ever-inebriated world, one in which he does constant battle with Bardolfo and Pistola, those sidekicks to whom he sings ironically of "honor." And in this low-life milieu Falstaff reappears in Act II, first to be visited by the ceremonious Dame Quickly, then in all his most hilarious finery to pay his call on Mistress Ford. The inner courtyard of the rustic Ford house immediately conveys a sense of everyday Elizabethan life with its sun-baked flowers, lines of drying laundry, second-story balcony on which the merry wives can read their letters from Falstaff and spy on Ford and his friends in pursuit of the amorous knight, and in which the young lovers can chase one another and echo their ardent love song. That same double-story structure serves for the Act II interior when Falstaff, as instructed by Quickly,

pays his call on Mistress Ford between the hours of 2 and 3 p.m. The comfortable Ford home boasts heavy wooden furniture, a large screen to hide Sir John from Ford and then to shield the kissing lovers, a large vase with flowers on a velvet-covered table, wood-and-plaster ceiling and walls, a delightful bay window of leaded glass looking out over the Thames—the ideal spot for the laundry basket filled with a hiding, cringing Falstaff to be dumped into the dirty river.

When the duped knight emerges in Act III, Scene 1, it is at the rear of the Garter Inn at sunset, a scene with an abandoned hay cart and wooden fencing, behind which the wives can spy on their subject. Finally comes the Windsor Park scene in the dead of night, with as its mysterious focal point, Herne's Oak, the massive tree around which Falstaff, wearing his antlers, is pursued and mocked for his irrepressible wooing. Here Zeffirelli creates a kind of dream Halloween with Nannetta, disguised as the queen of the fairies, making her entrance riding a donkey, attended by youthful spirits. The effect is enhanced by lit pumpkins giving out an eerie orange glow, throwing shadows that only add

to the general confusion in which the tricked Ford agrees to the marriage of Nannetta and Fenton.

At the same time, Zeffirelli's perceptive, literal direction endows each character with a clear identity, even in such details as the way they sit down on a piece of furniture. The robust Dame Quickly, whom Zeffirelli makes a second pivotal figure as the female counterpart of Falstaff, sits down like a great deflated balloon and ceremoniously pays her respects of "Reverenza" to Sir John with just enough pompous exaggeration to make fun of the knight and yet make him believe in her sincerity. As Regina Resnik, who sang the role of Quickly, has recalled apropos working with Zeffirelli, "It was just one long joy about character acting, how to play, be funny, enjoy your music. But it was hard getting around in that sixty-pound dress. I asked why the dress had to be so heavy, and he said, 'Because you will walk like you have bunions, and you will run like you have big tits.'"

Falstaff himself is made to walk with the grand swagger of someone who has known better, more prosperous, more honorable days, but still keeps up the illusion; and his sitting down becomes more an act of dropping himself onto any given piece of furniture. Together, Falstaff and Quickly match wits as lusty, good-humored, scheming veterans. Mistresses Ford and Page offer an aura of glamour as the merry wives in their Elizabethan finery and as the obvious objects of Sir John's lust. Nannetta and Fenton fly about in nonstop action oblivious to the rest of their world. Master Ford possesses a certain arrogance, panache, and dandyism in his style, while Falstaff's cohorts have just the right comic gusto and Elizabethan rowdiness. Each character is not only fully developed but also melded perfectly into the web of interpersonal relationships in this small-town background.

It is Falstaff who observes, "I am not only witty in myself but the cause of that wit is in other men." Zeffirelli catches Shakespeare's wit to perfection with his exquisite sense of timing and pacing. And if the ultimate theatrical experience is one that takes us away from our own existence and thrusts us into a world of make-believe, of fantasy, of other lives and times, then Zeffirelli's *Falstaff* provides music theater of the highest order.

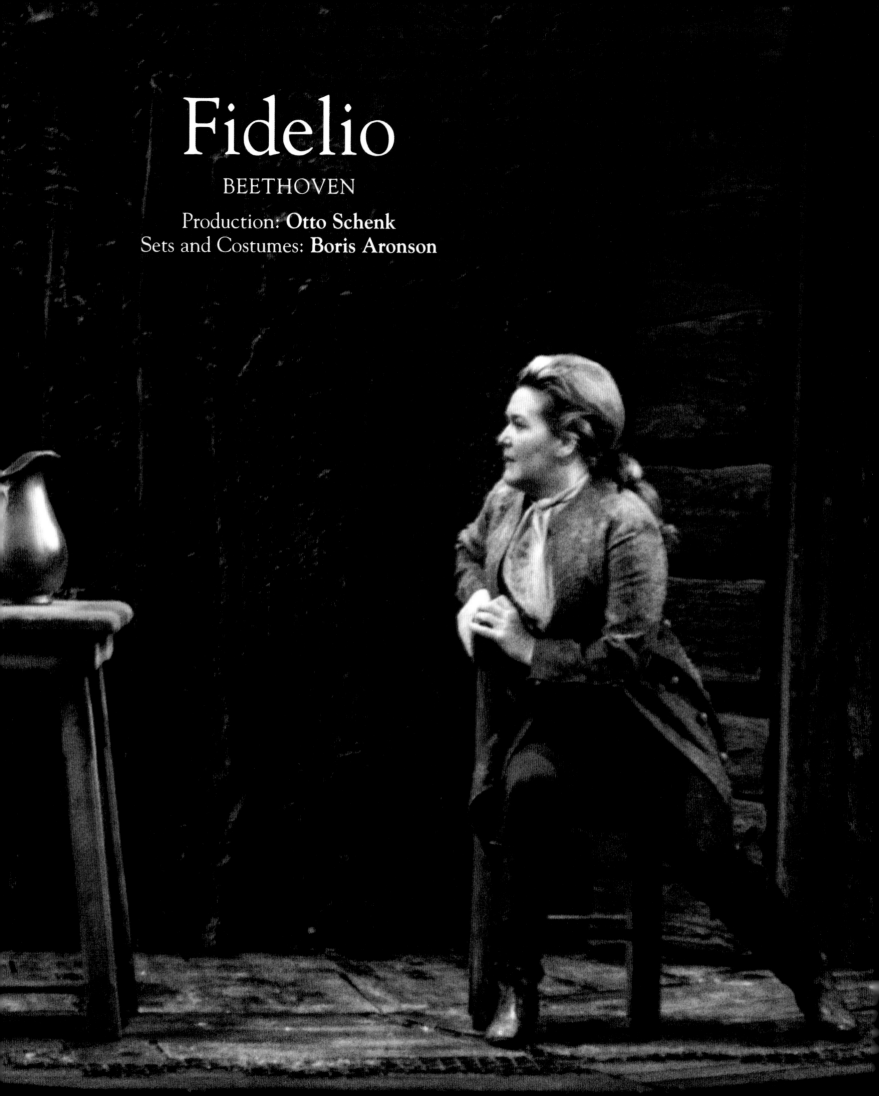

Fidelio

BEETHOVEN

Production: **Otto Schenk**
Sets and Costumes: **Boris Aronson**

Fidelio

BEETHOVEN's *Fidelio* is a stirring testament to the heroism and spirit of man. It is also a notoriously static work—one which is often barely tolerated because of its dramatic defects, but acceptable nevertheless because its composer happens to be Ludwig van Beethoven, and *Fidelio* his sole effort for the lyric theater. A heroic "rescue" opera, a fine example of a genre greatly in vogue in the late eighteenth and early nineteenth centuries, *Fidelio* is as much a political statement, a paean to liberty, as it is a testimony to the power of conjugal love, as portrayed in Leonore's unflinching resolve to free her husband Florestan from prison in a politically oppressed Spain. But this does not translate easily into suspenseful action or spellbinding theatrical effects, and over the years operagoers have had to endure all too many noble, high-minded, but inert performances of the work. However, when the Metropolitan Opera decided to stage *Fidelio* afresh to commemorate the 200th anniversary of Beethoven's birth in December 1970, it brought together a team of director, designer, conductor, and cast that made this timeless drama sizzle onstage. Critics deemed it the best-directed production of the work within living memory, and it quickly emerged as one of the major events in the worldwide Beethoven bicentennial celebrations.

While the libretto's late-eighteenth-century context is certainly suggested, there is a studied placelessness (nothing specifically Spanish) and timelessness about this production of *Fidelio*, for the universal application of the tale and its message can appeal directly to people of every country in every epoch, and of course Beethoven's music has the universal power to thrill and stir the emotions as well. The shackled, semi-hysterical wreck of Florestan, for example, could be any prisoner in any one of a thousand hellish dungeons where darkness and deprivation threaten to extinguish

hope. Veteran stage designer Boris Aronson (who has since died) was taking on his first opera in the standard repertory (he had first worked at the Met three years previously on the world premiere of Marvin David Levy's *Mourning Becomes Electra*), has conveyed the idea by creating a brooding, expressionistic set.

With some 109 Broadway credits to his name by 1970—including Archibald MacLeish's *J.B.* and such musicals as *Fiddler on the Roof* and *Cabaret*—Aronson said at the time that he saw opera as "a non-naturalistic art form that mustn't get lost in too many visual details." The style that he adopted for his grim, skeletal, unit-set *Fidelio* is characterized by features that evoke a moldering concentration camp: jagged, splintery, timbered beams and supports rotting with age (symbolic of the decaying political state); a looming iron gate separating the prison interior from the outside world; impenetrable stone walls; rough burlap for much of the clothing. In addition, as part of the scenic collage, he has heavy metal chains hanging in abstract sculptural form, a kind of octagonal central playing area of wide boards, secret niches above the stage for soldiers to patrol and spy from, waffled girders, and a mud-caked lath, all with a general *objet-trouvé* look and an air of dark menace.

In Scene 1, Marzelline is seen ironing on an improvised board in a room set off from the courtyard, its claustrophobic feeling created by the sight of elaborate gates to right and left. The rear walls of Rocco's living quarters then vanish, to reveal the cavernous yet oppressive courtyard, surrounded by impenetrable blackness and the barred gateway, beyond which—one is made to sense—lie the moat and bridge to freedom. The central circular playing area remains unchanged throughout, but after the first scene the stage lighting moves steadily, as does the action itself, from darkness to light, which is the very essence of *Fidelio*. Prisoners crawl out from spaces under the walls to take advantage of a few rays of sunlight that enter the courtyard, and, at the end of Act I, Leonore confronts the towering, barred, iron gate leading to the light-filled outer world with a combination of superhuman will, sad resignation, and overwhelming grief. At this point the task of finding her husband suddenly appears to present a struggle greater than she has ever imagined.

In Act II, Aronson adds a daunting central tower-staircase, which Rocco and Leonore descend, ostensibly to dig Florestan's grave. Florestan meanwhile lies chained at the foot of this rickety structure, with its curved stairs, by which the tyrant-governor Pizarro makes his dramatic entrance, with the intention of murdering Florestan—and then an even more dramatic exit. For the final scene, the tower is gone, but not the prison.

Above

At a rehearsal, director Otto Schenk works with Leonie Rysanek, who portrayed Leonore, and Walter Berry, who took the part of Pizarro in the original production in 1970.

◁ *Overleaf*

Act I, Scene 1. The jailer Rocco (Giorgio Tozzi) in his quarters with his daughter Marzelline (Judith Blegen) and the youth she hopes to marry, the newly hired assistant Fidelio—in fact Leonore (Leonie Rysanek) in disguise.

Light floods through the now transparent walls—a blinding white light, to which the long-suffering prisoners have to accustom their eyes as they greet their rough-clad wives, lovers, and families. The forces of light and Enlightenment have conquered those of darkness and repression. The colors used in Aronson's designs are gray-green and brown, but everything in the prison has a patina of age, mustiness, and gloom. "Stage dust," Aronson explained, "has to be cleaned up. The look of age can only be had by expert painting and fabric treatment. The prisoners wear ordinary clothes that seem to have undergone weeks and years of constant wear. The principals dress simply in dark colors. Pizarro's silhouette is more important in creating a figure of evil than any Nazi-type outfit." "My whole concept," he went on, "is closer to sculpture than to painting or architecture, and I always strive for consistency. . . . I tried in *Fidelio* for one style, based on the requirements of the musical and dramatic material."

The strongly etched humanity and human suffering that pervade this *Fidelio* and make it so meaningful are thanks to the exacting direction of Otto Schenk. Perhaps because of his own Viennese background and his experience as an actor, Schenk has been able to find just the right means to make the principal characters real, fusing them into a total musical-dramatic conception, their actions expressive of emotion and intelligence. The core of Schenk's approach was extremely simple: an ability to understand the characters of a work in the framework of the story. Yet he turns first not to the libretto, as might be expected, but to the score, because he feels that in the music there are often more clues to character, to meaning, and to movement. As to his method of working with singers and actors, Schenk, like Stanislavsky, suggests that it is not a "method" at all. "I'm not interested in *discussing* a role with a singer or actor. That's often a way to avoid working. I say, 'Show me!' If you ask a centipede how he walks with those hundred legs, if he thought about it he might not be able to walk anymore. So don't ask an actor or a singer too much about how he does it—or is going to do it. So much of what performers do is instinctive." Schenk's attitude to the inclusion of extraneous political content in his staging is a far cry from that of his fellow directors in the German-speaking theater today, for they tend to invest everything with heavy political and moral weight. Says Schenk, "If you put too much of today into an old opera or play, you ruin it. It isn't really about today, about our sensibilities. You have to say instead, 'Here is an old opera, full of passion, but see how many things in it still have meaning for us today.'"

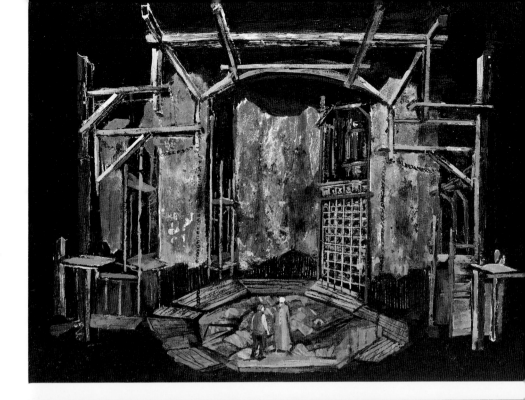

Above

Set designs by Boris Aronson for the prison courtyard (Act I, Scene 2) and the finale (Act II, Scene 2)—the transition from darkness to light.

Overleaf ▷

Act II, Scene 2. Leonore (Leonie Rysanek) and Rocco (Giorgio Tozzi) descend into the dungeon to prepare a grave for Pizarro's intended victim, the political prisoner Florestan (Jon Vickers), who lies in chains; earlier, Florestan (*right*), unjustly imprisoned, has seen a vision of his devoted wife Leonore.

Act I, Scene 2. The tyrannical governor, Don Pizarro (Donald McIntyre), resolves to kill his prisoner, Florestan—"Ha! welch' ein Augenblick." The plan will be thwarted, however, by the timely arrival of the minister, Don Fernando.

It was with these tenets that he approached *Fidelio* at the Met, on the heels of a Vienna State Opera production conducted by Leonard Bernstein. In New York, Schenk was fortunate enough to have Leonie Rysanek as Leonore and Jon Vickers as Florestan, both of whom rank as the world's leading exponents of their respective roles, having sung them in many of the world's opera houses and bringing to them an intensely personal, poignant commitment. What he did was only to intensify the singers' work onstage, refining it and giving it his particular focus. One of the most difficult aspects of *Fidelio* is the fact that a dramatic soprano (usually a mature woman) has to be disguised as a young man in order to gain entry to the prison in which, possibly, her husband is held. However, in a long coat and riding breeches, Rysanek looked the part to perfection, a dramatic white streak in her hair conveying a sense of aging in her psychological agony about finding Florestan. Schenk encouraged her to walk with a heavy, slightly bent, downtrodden gait that would communicate the tortured, distraught weariness in her mission, along with its overwhelming sense of helplessness.

The director's stroke of genius comes at the climax of the Act II prison scene, which becomes a crescendo of pathos and tension after Leonore has hidden herself on Pizarro's appearance. After confronting him with her pistol just as the trumpet announces the arrival of the minister, Don Fernando, and having forced Pizarro to return up the tortuous steps before be can murder Florestan, Leonore (in Rysanek's taut body) simply collapses at the foot of those tower steps on the chord of resolution in the orchestra—as if the strings of a puppet had suddenly been cut—her body slumping lifeless. When slowly, haltingly, Florestan asks her, "Was hast du für mich gelitten?," and she then tearfully replies, "Nichts, nichts, mein Florestan," the action reaches its almost unbearable, heart-wrenching denouement. This keen sense of theater, which has been magnificently plotted through Beethoven's score, now allows for a smooth transition to the inclusion of the *Leonore* Overture No. 3. Then in the final scene of transfiguration, when Leonore frees Florestan's long-fettered hands, the reunited couple join in the general hymn of rejoicing. Truly, Leonore emerges as Everywoman, Florestan as Everyman, in this dynamic narrative. Indeed, all the characters spring vividly to life. Marzelline is no simpering fool of a daughter, but a tough (even shrewish), strong-willed, hard-working, perspiring, young woman who knows her mind perfectly well, desiring this intense young man, Fidelio, and not the all-too available and compliant Jacquino. Rocco possesses a certain gruff warmth, but is always full of obvious greed, not only in his "gold" aria but in his subservient, eager-to-please, cowardly dealings with Pizarro. The evil prison governor, played in a close-cropped blond wig and long gray, Wehrmacht-style coat with wide lapels, comes across as a smoothly repellent villain, accompanied by a machine-drilled robot ensemble of soldiers straight out of Goya. Putting on his wire-framed glasses to read the letter, Pizarro is no hammy villain, but cruelty incarnate, a composite of all menacing, despotic oppressors from the beginning of time—tight-lipped, squint-eyed, the ideal product of the political system he serves. The chorus too is directed to maximum effect, the male prisoners, as they emerge from the dark depths, barely able to cope with their brief moment of freedom, air, light.

This *Fidelio* possesses that sense of fiery drama that always seemed latent in the score and libretto, but which rarely surfaces in performance. It is three-dimensional human drama on a grand scale—a testimony to everyone concerned in the production, and especially to Karl Böhm, whose heartfelt, intense conducting of Beethoven's only opera in its first season made it the pinnacle of his Met career.

Above and right
Act II, Scene 2. In the joyous finale, Leonore (Hildegard Behrens) prepares to release the chains of her husband, Florestan (James King), as Rocco (Kurt Moll) addresses Don Fernando (Bernd Weikl), and good triumphs over evil, personified by Pizarro (Siegmund Nimsgern); and, free at last, Florestan (Jon Vickers) embraces Leonore (Hildegard Behrens).

Francesca da Rimini

ZANDONAI

Production: **Piero Faggioni**   Sets: **Ezio Frigerio**
Costumes: **Franca Squarciapino**   Lighting: **Gil Wechsler**

Francesca da Rimini

ONE OF the Met's principal objectives from the time James Levine took up the post of Music Director in 1976 has been to rediscover older operas which, for one reason or another, have fallen out of the mainstream repertory. Works of this kind can still be fascinating on many levels, even though they will never be part of the regular diet. One of these is Riccardo Zandonai's *Francesca de Rimini* of 1914, a plush melodrama which was staged by the Met for two seasons in 1916–18, with Frances Alda and Giovanni Martinelli in the principal roles. American exposure to the work in the intervening years had been virtually nonexistent, although Italian theaters continue to keep it on the boards with some regularity. In spite of the extravagant, high-flown, even morbid libretto by Gabriele D'Annunzio (he created his original play as a vehicle for his then mistress, Eleonora Duse, who triumphed in the title role), it is a work that will thrive whenever the audience can make its way through the morass of poetic language and the ambience of gaudy grandiloquence that form part of D'Annunzio's bizarre cult-of-the-beautiful aesthetic. Zandonai's lush score, too, remains a special taste, a compendium of everything that was in the air before World War I—*verismo*, Richard Strauss, Wagner, Debussy, *et al.* But it lacks a strong individual profile, except for its occasional bombast, and provides no real emotional or even vocal climaxes. Each act unfolds in prolonged atmospheric scene-setting, while the undramatized emotional content boils in the symphonic declarations of the orchestra. This story of doom-laden love does not really get into anything like high gear until Act II. There are also enormous demands on the artists in the two leading roles, Francesca and Paolo, which require great singing qualities in the phrasing of the poetic text, as well as grand heroic voices to carry Zandonai's punishing vocal line and to project through his dense, colorful orchestration.

For the Met in 1984 it was an act of sheer but exquisite extravagance to invest a healthy purse and much creative talent in reviving a work that seems, at most, to warrant only periodic exploration. This production of *Francesca da Rimini* was given one of the most opulent and costly mountings in recent times, the kind of massive, picturesque, richly detailed, romantic staging that draws audible oohs and aahs from the audience as the curtain rises for each act.

Right

Act I. In the courtyard of the Polenta family's palazzo in Ravenna, the jester Simonetto (Brian Schexnayder) prepares to recount Arthurian tales to Francesca's attendants, but will be thwarted by more important business.

◁ *Overleaf*

Act III. Paolo (Placido Domingo) and Francesca (Renata Scotto), reading the tale of Lancelot and Guinevere, surrender to adulterous love.

Left
Act I. Francesca (Renata Scotto) gives a rose to the handsome Paolo (Placido Domingo), whom she mistakenly believes to be her betrothed. Earlier, Francesca, about to leave home, has comforted her sister Samaritana (Nicole Lorange).

Set design by Ezio Frigerio for the courtyard of the Polenta palace in Ravenna (Act I).

Above

Act I. The lawyer Ser Toldo (Anthony Laciura) and Francesca's brother Ostasio (Richard Fredricks) plot a marriage by proxy for the girl.

Opposite

Act III. As Francesca (Renata Scotto) reclines on her couch, her friends—Garsenda (Gail Robinson), Biancofiore (Natalia Rom), Donella (Claudia Catania), and Altichiara (Gail Dubinbaum)—sing in praise of spring, as dancers hold doves.

Among the ingredients stirred into this grand, complex mixture is the tradition of courtly love, stemming from the twelfth century and continuing into the early Renaissance, when important marriages were invariably made for political reasons. Adulterous courtly love was the only alternative to these loveless alliances entered into by members of the nobility. Italian poets made their own variation on this in the *dolce stile nuovo*, or "sweet new style," in which the woman became spiritualized and idealized into a *donna angelicata*, a woman made angel-like. Later, visual artists would explore aspects of the lovers' physicality and carnality as well, among them Dante Gabriel Rossetti, the Pre-Raphaelite painter and poet named for his illustrious Italian predecessor. D'Annunzio described his *Francesca da Rimini* as a "poema di sangue et di lussuria," a poem of blood and lust. Many elements of courtly love are evident both in the play and in the opera; and Francesca herself, adored by Paolo as an unearthly vision, nevertheless exerts a fatal sex appeal.

The production team for this staging was led by one of Italy's leading directors, Piero Faggioni, and included Ezio Frigerio as designer, together with the latter's wife, Franca Squarciapino, as costume designer. All three were making their debut at the Met, but Faggioni had worked in opera for twenty years, having started at La Fenice in Venice with *La Bohème* in 1964. Born in Carrara, he studied at the National Academy of Dramatic Art in Rome and began his career as an actor. As an opera director, he has staged *Manon Lescaut* and *Tosca* for La Scala, *La Fanciulla del West* for Covent Garden and at the Teatro Colón in Buenos Aires, *Norma* for the Vienna State Opera, *Samson et Dalila* for the Paris Opéra, *Carmen* for the Edinburgh Festival, and *Macbeth* for the Salzburg Festival, as well as many productions in Venice. He has frequently collaborated with Frigerio in these projects, but among the latter's other credits are designs for productions at the Paris Opéra, La Scala, the Vienna State Opera, the Rome Opera, the Teatro San Carlo in Naples, the Lyric Opera of Chicago, Covent Garden, as well as the Salzburg Festival.

The all-Italian team of Faggioni, Frigerio, and Squarciapino manage to take the vast background of the opera in hand and to give the work an unfailing sense of unity. Frigerio achieves a meaningful balance between the splendor and asceticism of medieval Ravenna and Rimini (the towns in which the opera is set) and the Pre-Raphaelite sensuality of the score and D'Annunzio's poetry. He devised darkly polished marble-like walls which remain a constant element for the Polenta and Malatesta castles. In a subtle symbolic touch, these are made to move in on Paolo and Francesca

The story of Paolo and Francesca has its roots in the thirteenth century, when Dante immortalized them in his *Divine Comedy*; there we find the tormented couple among the Lustful in the Second Circle of Hell. Painters, writers, and musicians have frequently been drawn to these star-crossed lovers, whose fame in literary history is surpassed only by Romeo and Juliet and Tristan and Isolde. Literary associations abound. For one thing, it is while reading the medieval romance of Lancelot and Guinevere that Paolo and Francesca indeed fall in love, as that story excites their erotic daydreaming. For another, the languid, late-Romantic spirit of Wagner's *Tristan und Isolde* hangs over the Italian opera, infusing it with a *fin-de-siècle* hothouse atmosphere.

from act to act as their fatal entrapment and mutual absorption are played out, only to part again with a shaft of light after their murder by Gianciotto and the committing of their souls to an eternal inferno. Frigerio creates extravagant pictures of an imaginary age, Pre-Raphaelite in feeling, poetically laden with flowers, tapers, a Gothic tower for the bloody, violent Act II battle, and a glowing stained-glass window for Francesca's chamber.

Squarciapino's costumes are ideally suited to this spectacular vision, the women in flowing silken dresses which not only capture a sense of storybook fantasy, but possess a symbolic function: Francesca's gowns progress from pale pastels to violent red as the action proceeds and as her love for Paolo evolves into something increasingly physical. In his handling of this hybrid work, Faggioni shows his mettle with a graceful but strongly focused and purposeful stage presentation exhibiting an appropriate period flavor. Much of the acting is not in the naturalistic or veristic vein, but poetically stylized, except in the scenes of violence and in the powerful confrontation between Gianciotto and Malatestino. Otherwise, Faggioni has chosen to fill scenes with long, significant gazes between the tension-filled principals, and reveals a thorough understanding of the sex and violence at play in *Francesca*. Only occasionally is the heroine (Renata Scotto was cast in the title role) encouraged to indulge in an overwrought massaging of her loins to convey the girl's budding sexual desire, but otherwise the production is a model of poetry and refinement.

Overleaf ▷
Act II. During the heat of battle with the Ghibelines, Gianciotto (Cornell MacNeil) looks down from the ramparts of the Malatesta castle at his wife Francesca (Renata Scotto) below. Viewing the combat are Gianciotto (*above, right*) and the troubled Francesca with Paolo (Placido Domingo), to whom she has given a goblet of wine.

Act I of *Francesca da Rimini* is nearly all dreamlike in atmosphere, preparing the audience for the fateful meeting of the handsome Paolo, who has been sent from Ravenna to Rimini to represent his brother—the lame, deformed Gianciotto—and Francesca, who is to marry Gianciotto but who, on seeing Paolo, mistakenly believes it is he who will be her future husband. Not unlike the presentation of the silver rose in the Strauss-Hofmannsthal *Der Rosenkavalier*, Francesca plucks a single red rose from a bush and offers it to the young nobleman, almost as a symbol of giving up her virginity to him. The curtain falls on a scene of enchantment, as love is kindled between the young pair without either of them uttering a word—only their eyes meet.and become transfixed. An offstage chorus of women floats a sensuous melody over a ravishing orchestral texture of shimmering strings, punctuated by the archaic sounds of a lute, *piffero* (fife), and throbbing *viola pomposa*, as Francesca hands Paolo the rose. This delicate mood painting, courtesy of Zandonai, finds ideal expression in Faggioni's sensitive handling of the scene, combined with Frigerio's two-level set, suggestive of elegance and glowing languorousness. Paolo is first seen through golden grillework as the lovers-to-be remain spellbound, enraptured.

But the other side of the Zandonai–D'Annunzio coin comes in Act II, playing out its ferocious battle scene between the Guelphs and Ghibelines on a sinister multi-level Constructivist citadel filled with trap doors, drawbridges, ramps, projectiles, battering ram, fireballs, and crossbow arrows sent flying amid much brutality and confusion. Here, Paolo is injured and Francesca tends his wound as their delicate love begins to grow amid the realities of violence.

Francesca's atmospheric bedroom appropriately suggests her isolation from the rest of the world, with its medieval book stand, candelabra, stained-glass window, out of which her attendants flutter paper doves in one of the most delightful moments of Faggioni's staging. Here, in Act III, the lovers' repressed sexual attraction turns increasingly physical, evolving in choreographed fashion into a gripping sequence of strongly picturesque visual images. And it is in this lavish, magical, private kingdom that the lovers are eventually undone, as they become fatally entrapped by Gianciotto. The latter has been advised of the affair by still another brother, Malatestino, suitably nicknamed the "One-Eyed." The fleeing Paolo catches his cloak on the trap door and is savagely murdered by the crazed Gianciotto.

The audience is drawn into a strange, faraway world through the power and visual beauty of this monumental production, which successfully supports and unifies all the elements that make up Zandonai's setting of D'Annunzio's flamboyant drama.

Left and opposite
Act IV, Scene 1. The angry Gianciotto (Cornell MacNeil, right) threatens to kill his brother Malatestino, the "One-Eyed" (William Lewis), if he has lied in telling him that Paolo is Francesca's lover; and the bloodthirsty Malatestino takes an ax, the weapon he uses offstage to silence a prisoner in the dungeon.

Die Frau ohne Schatten

STRAUSS

Production: **Nathaniel Merrill**
Sets and Costumes: **Robert O'Hearn**

Die Frau ohne Schatten

WHEN the Metropolitan Opera transferred to Lincoln Center in the fall of 1966, Rudolf Bing planned a mighty celebration of new productions to show off his company and the latest technical wizardry that was available to it in the new theater; the previous lack of technical facilities, as well as storage and building space, had been one of the main considerations in the decision to move up Broadway from West 39th Street. The opening fell to Samuel Barber's commissioned *Antony and Cleopatra*, designed and directed in gargantuan, smothering style by Franco Zeffirelli. Immediately following it came Ponchielli's *La Gioconda* (directed by Margarita Wallmann, designed by Beni Montresor) and Verdi's *La Traviata* (directed by Alfred Lunt, designed by Cecil Beaton). Theatrical spectacle ruled the day, but it was Richard Strauss's *Die Frau ohne Schatten* which emerged as the revelation of the season's festivities. This towering work by Strauss and his longtime collaborator Hugo von Hofmannsthal was having its New York stage premiere, only the second production ever in the United States (the first having been staged in San Francisco in 1959, forty years after the opera's world premiere in Vienna).

Bing had been urged on for several years by Leonie Rysanek to produce *Die Frau ohne Schatten* (Rysanek stands as the most celebrated Empress in the work's history to date), but he rightly waited until he had a theater that could satisfactorily accommodate such large-scale fantasy, for this opera needs the kind of facilities that only the new Met could provide: a turntable, stage elevators, and large side stages with vast rear stage space. Not only did Strauss's music, as authoritatively con-

ducted by the venerable Karl Böhm (a close colleague of the composer's), grip the imagination of the audiences, but the settings by Robert O'Hearn and direction by Nathaniel Merrill more than honored what Strauss and Hofmannsthal demanded in their modern, psychological, fantastc fairy tale. As Harold C. Schonberg wrote in the *New York Times* following the Met premiere, "It would not be overstressing the point to say that [this] . . . is the most elaborate production ever put on by the company . . . The opera is a big, spectacular work, and the Metropolitan went all-out in its presentation. Everything was used. Sets came forward and went back; sets rose into the air or descended into the bowels of the earth. There was smoke; there was a fountain; the voice of the Falcon came from the top of the auditorium . . . Robert O'Hearn's sets and costumes, and Nathaniel Merrill's staging, were a unity, and a more lavish approach to the stage has not been seen in our time. For once at the Metropolitan, a convincing union between literalism and modernism was achieved."

The Merrill–O'Hearn team had become one of Bing's favored production forces at the Met after their joint debut there in 1961 with Donizetti's *L'Elisir d'amore*. On the way to the scale of *Die Frau ohne Schatten* they had fielded with distinction such epics as Wagner's *Die Meistersinger von Nürnberg*, Verdi's *Aida*, and Saint-Saëns' *Samson et Dalila*. Both men brought vast experience to the Met. Massachusetts-born Merrill began as a college math major, but switched to musicology and studied stage direction with Boris Goldovsky at the New England Conservatory, where he came under the spell of opera. Later he received a James Reynolds Graduate Fellowship from Dartmouth to study opera production in Germany in 1953; subsequently, he was assistant director at the Hamburg State Opera and at the Hessisches Staatstheater in Wiesbaden, and also worked in Bremen and Kiel. Other assignments took him to Glyndebourne and Salzburg before a Washington, D.C., *Don Giovanni* with sets by O'Hearn was seen by Bing, who brought both men to the Met for the Donizetti comic opera. The Indiana-born O'Hearn studied at Indiana University and the Arts Students' League in New York before gaining experience with designer Donald Oenslager and working on some sixty productions at the Brattle Theater in Cambridge, Massachusetts. The first opera he designed, for Sarah Caldwell at Boston University, was Verdi's *Falstaff*, after which he put his hand to *The Rake's Progress*. Having assisted Oliver Smith with several Broadway shows, as well as the Met's 1957 *La Traviata*, he teamed up with Merrill for many productions at Central City, Colorado, and the Opera Society of Washington.

Both men approach their task on two simple premises: that in opera the stage direction should spring from the music, and that grand opera exists to be sung. As Merrill has said, "My main function as stage director is to place singers in the position onstage where they can be most comfortable for singing. Opera music is written for things to happen by—if possible happenings the composer wanted. Sometimes the directions are clear in the score. Sometimes the composer himself wasn't convinced and had to learn in rehearsal, so that everybody knew what they were doing but nothing was written down. I conceive an opera staging as a music form. The music is all-determining. Opera provides a totally different emotional experience from the theater, stemming from the music and the singers. Music dictates the exact seconds of time singers have to get from one place to another. I am a devotee of 'grand' opera. I love big stage movements." Merrill's collaborations with O'Hearn have long been close, and for them not only is the essential conception of the work to be performed at stake, but the arrangement of physical space onstage must be in accordance with the action required by the plot. As in all successful production teams, the two men seem to share a kind of ESP in knowing what they want to achieve onstage, and how to do it.

Above

Act I, Scene 2. Inside the Dyer's house, the Nurse (Irene Dalis) tells the Wife (Christa Ludwig) how she may obtain a life of luxury.

Overleaf ▷

Act I, Scene 1. The Nurse (Irene Dalis) outside the imperial palace.
Act III, Scene 3 (*inset*). The Emperor (James King), whose life has been saved, with the Empress (Leonie Rysanek), who has earned her shadow.

Act II, Scene 4. The Empress (Leonie Rysanek) realizes in a dream that she has done Barak (Walter Berry) a terrible wrong.

What they achieved with *Die Frau ohne Schatten* was a culmination of the postwar interest in what Strauss called his "child of sorrow," a work that represented eight years of hard labor on his and Hofmannsthal's part. There had previously been celebrated stagings in Munich, Hamburg, and Vienna; and then in the aftermath of the Met's widely hailed production came new stagings, including those at Covent Garden, in Paris, and again in San Francisco. Production styles have varied from the vividly realistic to the totally abstract, and the Met's straddled these two in a delicate balance. As O'Hearn commented at the time, this is one of the most difficult operas to design since it takes place not just in a fantasy world but in *three* fantasy worlds. "It has not one but two stories to tell," he observed, "the fairy-tale one we see and hear, and a very elaborate philosophical one running neck and neck with it. The real meanings are purposely hidden and the clues confused, so the designer must venture on a detective hunt."

This opera presents any number of challenges to create stage magic—a flood, sudden appearances and disappearances, fish that fly into a pan, visions, a shadow that turns into a bridge, and a shadow—that of the Empress—which must not be seen until the climactic moment. Hofmannsthal stressed that this opera would stand in the same relation to Mozart's *Die Zauberflöte* as *Der Rosenkavalier* does to *Le Nozze di Figaro*; and indeed the two works are concerned with a solemn religious world alongside a fairy-tale realm, together with a stern but benevolent divine force (represented by the spirit ruler Keikobad in *Die Frau*, by the high priest Sarastro in *Die Zauberflöte*), as well as the use of magic tricks and trials to prove the couples' worthiness in their union.

An extraordinary number of decisions have to be made in realizing such a grand-scale, demanding work. Notable among them is the question: how realistic or how stylized and symbolic should it be? Merrill and O'Hearn began with that invaluable source, the vast correspondence between composer and librettist, along with Hofmannsthal's original prose version of the story, which helps to illuminate many details that are simply ignored in the libretto or have been pruned away. The team had to search for the underlying meanings and theme of the work. "*Die Frau*," says O'Hearn, "exists on two parallel levels. It has the surface fairy-tale story, vaguely Far Eastern, and the hidden theme of the acquiring of humanity—the shadow of fertility, which the Empress seeks." He followed Hofmannsthal's delineation of the Empress as having a "threefold nature, part animal, part human, and part spirit. Only the animal and spirit aspects are apparent in the first scene. In between there is a vacuum: the humanity is missing. To acquire this humanity—that is the meaning of the whole work. At the end the animal and spirit aspects appear fused in a new being on a higher plane." Primary for the designer is the existence of three worlds—the spirit world, the world of men, and the in-between limbo of the Emperor and Empress.

Above and left

Act III, Scene 3. The Emperor (James King) turns to stone, only his eyes still able to communicate. When the Empress (Leonie Rysanek) refuses to drink from the fountain, she saves him.

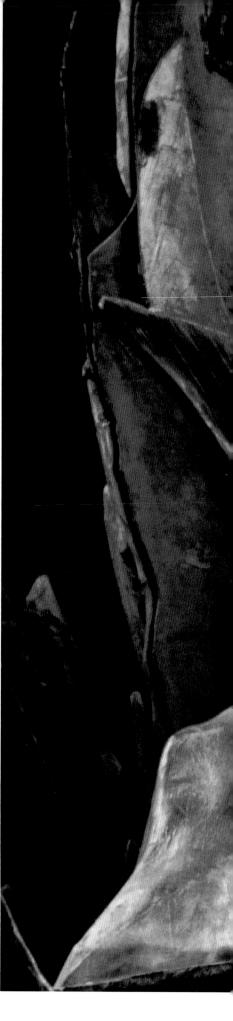

Above
Set designs by Robert O'Hearn for Act III, Scenes 1 and 2.

Act III, Scene 3. The finale, with the Empress (Eva Marton) and the Emperor (Gerd Brenneis) above a waterfall, and below them Barak (Franz Ferdinand Nentwig) and his Wife (Birgit Nilsson).

O'Hearn took into account many of the librettist's thoughts about the work being "a many-colored spectacle with palace and hut, priests, boats, torches, tunnels through rock, choruses, children," and that its "meaning is always to be found between the two great images, LIGHT and DARKNESS, and when these meet the SHADOW is formed." To give variety to the three visits to the Dyer's hut in Act II, Hofmannsthal declared, "the imagination of the scene-painter will have to come to our aid here." O'Hearn and Merrill looked at photos of earlier productions as well as the older Sievert and Preetorius designs. Ultimately, they decided that the work should be set in no specific country. "Rather," as O'Hearn described it, "the design should reflect the mood and meaning of each scene and world: a bluish icy-cold, glassy, jeweled world for the Empress, a warm red-earthy world of men for the Dyer, Barak, and his steaming vats, a black-and-silver world of iridescent rock and winglike forms for the spirits. Also, water—physically and symbolically, the water of life—is important from the first utterance of the Nurse on and should be shown as shimmering light reflections from water and fountains."

With the exciting new world of stage mechanisms in the new theater, they decided to place the Dyer's house underneath the double lift, with the Empress's glassy world above, so that these two planes would retain their physical relationship to each other onstage. The spirit world was to be set up on the revolving part of the rear stage, so that it would move fluidly from one of the many scenes to another. In Act III, for the transition from the cave temple to the final landscape, the scenery would revolve through 180° in full view of the audience, from darkness to light. As O'Hearn explained, "Because the four singers do little but stand and sing for six minutes, we use the scenery itself to provide movement, at the very end having the entire set recede slowly upstage." In plot and mood, Act II moves from light to darkness, Act III from darkness to light. For the latter, O'Hearn planned a progression through the color spectrum, starting with black and purple for the grotto and going through blue to green to yellow-green to golden yellow for the final burst of daylight and the deliverance of Emperor and Empress to a human, child-bearing existence.

While the set for the Dyer's hut conveyed a certain feeling of earthly reality, the remainder of the production dispensed with any equally realistic treatment of Eastern temples. Instead, O'Hearn turned to enlarged photos of microscopic organisms and minerals, studies of jewels and branched quartz. He searched for such unusual materials as transparent plastics and those with oily, iridescent surfaces. The Dyer's house became a sculptural

abstraction, something like the inside of a broken clay pot lit by a volcanic fireplace. Notes the designer, "In other words, relevant forms based on nature superseded real period detail to bring out the basic motives. The veined texture of the curved walls was suggested by a photo blow-up of the eye of a frog." In creating the all-important three-dimensional scale models of each of the twelve scenes (once the sketches had been finalized), O'Hearn tried to use the unconventional materials subsequently used for the real sets: plastics, crushed glass, jewels, crinkled metal-foil surfaces, and so on.

Costumes, too, shed any feeling of precise country or period, but each became right for a specific character, from the Empress's floating blue gown with its crystalline headdress in Scene 1, to the Nurse's sinister black with its satanic red suggestions in the skirt panels, to the drab burlap basics of the Dyer and his Wife. Added to this was a magical sense of lighting in distinguishing the three worlds, together with the all-important projections on various levels of scrims from front to back. At the outset, as the Emperor's cool, airy, evanescent terrace of Scene 1 vanishes into the flies, to be replaced by the lowly, steaming dwelling of the Dyer, one can sense the physical descent of the Empress and the Nurse into the world of man, where they will seek the crucial shadow before the Emperor turns to stone, as decreed by Keikobad. Thanks to artful use of the stage elevators, one can also experience, in Act II, the flight of the Empress back to her bedchamber where, in an elegantly hung bed, she will experience her nightmares about the Emperor turning to stone. And stage elevators make the climax of Act II a chilling experience as the earth opens up, separating Barak and his Wife, and bringing chaos into their already calamitous world. The separate grottoes of Act III, where Barak and his mate search for one another and then sing of their mutual love, give way to the boat that has brought the Nurse and the Empress to the rocky terrace leading to Keikobad's monumental temple; there, the Empress banishes her Nurse forever, damning her to live among men for eternity. The Empress mounts the steps, bravely enters the temple, and arrives at the vast room with its golden fountain that is to decide her own and the Emperor's destiny. Torn between wanting the wife's shadow and desperate to save her husband, who gradually turns to stone, she declares, "I will not drink!" In making this personal sacrifice, the Empress has been severely tested, and Keikobad rewards her with her shadow, just as he liberates the Emperor so that the couple can be reunited. O'Hearn's gigantic revolving set begins turning as the scene brightens, and the Empress's shadow is trans-

formed into that proscribed golden bridge that serves to bring the Dyer and his Wife together again at a waterfall. The royal couple stand high over this earthly pair as all four sing of their love and listen to the voices of the children about to be born to both of them. Light has vanquished darkness, man and woman have found their ideal relationship, just as Strauss and Hofmannsthal had envisioned. Thanks to the practical application of Merrill's motto of approaching an opera through its music and through what its creators intended and demanded, this now-historic production at the Met remains one of the most authentic and emotionally charged conceptions of the opera yet seen.

The Met's intricate stage machinery in use during a rehearsal for Act I: the set for Scene 1 rises on an elevator, to be replaced by the Dyer's house in Scene 2, which is lifted from below stage level.

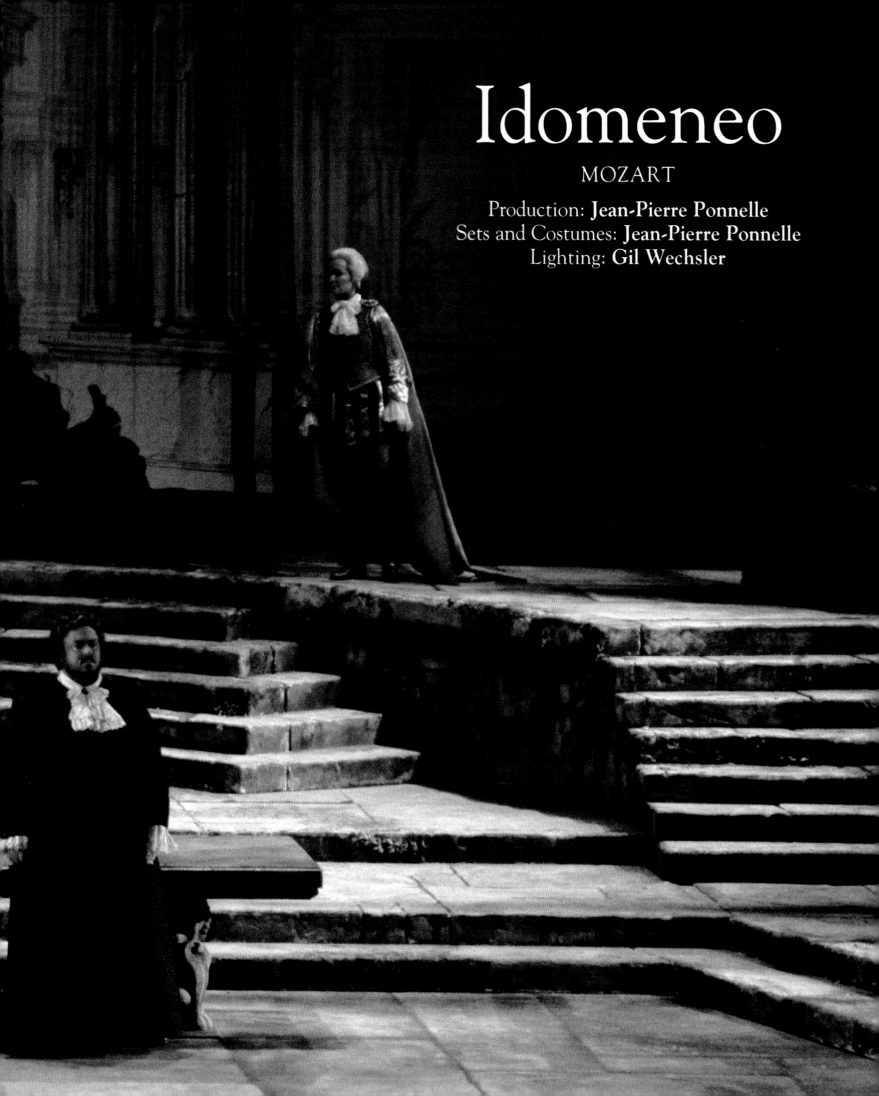

Idomeneo

MOZART

Production: **Jean-Pierre Ponnelle**
Sets and Costumes: **Jean-Pierre Ponnelle**
Lighting: **Gil Wechsler**

Idomeneo

PROBABLY more than any other opera director-designer today, Jean-Pierre Ponnelle has helped to shape and lead an international aesthetic, not only because of the prodigious number of his productions in theaters throughout Europe and America—from Salzburg, Milan, and Vienna to Chicago, San Francisco, and the Metropolitan—but even more importantly because of the dozen or so productions he has directed for television, screened regularly on European and American TV networks. No international house of any standing would think of being without a Ponnelle staging, and although his tastes extend in time from Monteverdi through Henze, he has concentrated to a large degree on works by Mozart and Rossini. In general he looks on opera as "the greatest artistic expression of Western civilization."

Born in 1932 in Paris, Ponnelle spent his youth in Burgundy, and after World War II his family moved to Germany—to Baden-Baden, where his father was head of the SWF Radio station in the French occupation zone. Later, Ponnelle studied at the Sorbonne: painting under Fernand Léger, philosophy and art history, as well as music with Hans Rosbaud in exchange for French lessons. With that French-German connection still a strong force in his youth, and having learned design as assistant to Carl Ebert, he met Hans Werner Henze and became involved in designing sets for the world premiere in 1952 of that composer's first full-length opera, *Boulevard Solitude*, an updated version of the Manon Lescaut story. Its success paved the way to a full-time career in the theater, first in the 1950s as a designer of ballet, opera, and theater in Austria, Germany, France, and Italy. In 1958 Kurt Herbert Adler brought him to America to design Carl Orff's *Carmina Burana* for the San Francisco Opera, the success of which led to Ponnelle's production of the American premiere of Strauss's *Die Frau ohne Schatten* there. After two-and-a-half years of French military service in Algeria, he decided that

if he was to realize his full conception in the theater he would have to direct as well as design, and in 1961 he began with nothing less than Wagner's *Tristan und Isolde*. On a practical level, he says, having the same person devise the sets and the direction simply saves time and money. But he realizes the problem inherent in such a dual role (though that trend has been increasing in opera in recent years): the lack of a partner for dialogue, since a certain amount of fighting and arguing can be productive for the final result. But the dialogue he finds instead in his collaboration with conductors of strong theatrical personality, and there are few major maestros of our time with whom Ponnelle has not worked in some fashion.

One of Ponnelle's strongest virtues—and most cherishable qualities at the same time—is his impeccable musicality as a director-designer. He works directly from the orchestral score in developing his ideas. "The main thing," he insists, "is to do nothing against the music and never smother the music with the story." Even before he begins the practical designs, Ponnelle outlines his basic concept of a work, a concept based wholly on the music. He analyzes the score, and most singers who work with him recognize the fact that he is musically infallible. Looking at a score, he can see the dramatic sense inherent in the notes, the musical phrases—everything that appears in the printed score.

"Mozart," declares Ponnelle unequivocally, "is my first and last love. I have done all his operas, including *Lucio Silla* and *Mitridate, Re di Ponto*. No note in Mozart is ever wrong, from the first to the last. Even the modulations make dramatic sense. It is a totally moral world. I feel when I start to work on a Mozart opera that he is so close to the conductor, to the director, to the singers through the notes, his printed symbols. Mozart is always right, and he is never boring. In so many arias he does the opposite of what you expect in showing the human dimension, and he is always right."

Above

Director and conductor in conversation—Jean-Pierre Ponnelle with James Levine; and (*right*) design by Jean-Pierre Ponnelle for the Cretan seashore in Act I.

◁ *Overleaf*

Act II, Scene 1. In the palace, the Trojan princess Ilia (Ileana Cotrubas) sings the aria "Se il padre" to Idomeneo (Luciano Pavarotti), while his son Idamante (Frederica Von Stade) listens.

This passion for Mozart has led to many different Ponnelle productions of the composer's most popular operas—*Le Nozze di Figaro*, *Così fan tutte*, *Don Giovanni*, *Die Zauberflöte*—as well as the two examples of opera seria that seem to form bookends to Mozart's operatic writing, *Idomeneo, Re di Creta*, and *La Clemenza di Tito*. Ponnelle has produced both of these works at the Met, the former in 1982, the latter in 1984. In each case these were premieres with the company, one just before, the other just after the Met's centenary season, and both were presented in a similar, highly stylized fashion. Ponnelle had previously produced *Idomeneo* elsewhere—including Cologne, Zurich, and Salzburg, as well as a staging shared by Chicago and San Francisco in the late 1970s. And the success of his Met productions of *Idomeneo* and *La Clemenza di Tito* was due to an elegant, detailed period style, allied with an emotionally cogent ensemble, full of vigor and richness. Both productions seemed to challenge the eye and the mind along with the emotions, and in an opera house one can ask for little more.

Above and left
Act I, Scene 2. Safely on land after the terrors of the storm, Idomeneo (Luciano Pavarotti) has a vision of Neptune; earlier, he has arrived in Sidon with his followers.

Act III. (*Opposite*) Elettra (Hildegard Behrens) in her final outburst "D'Oreste, d'Aiace," as Idomeneo (Luciano Pavarotti) looks on, and (*below*) Ilia (Ileana Cotrubas) calls upon the breezes to bear her love to Idamante—"Zeffiretti lusinghieri."
(*Right*) Idomeneo (Luciano Pavarotti), who gives his kingdom of Crete to Ilia and Idamante.

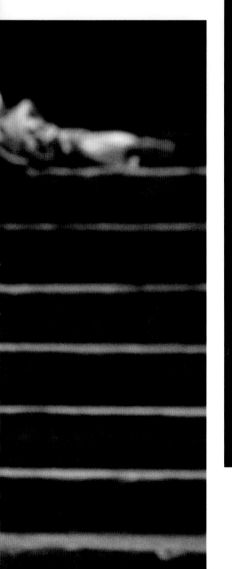

Opposite

Act II, Scene 3. Idamante (Frederica Von Stade), about to set sail with Elettra for Greece, takes leave of his father, Idomeneo (Luciano Pavarotti).

Moments of greatness or near-greatness occur so infrequently that when they do they are unmistakable. For the Met premiere of Mozart's *Idomeneo* in October 1982, 201 years after this *dramma eroico*'s original first night in Munich, the theater brought together an all-star cast in the principal roles, and under Ponnelle's direction the various elements were fused into a brilliant experience, grand in scale and scope, full of tragic outbursts and pathos, keeping the audience riveted for nearly four hours. This is no easy task, given the underlying opera-seria format, with its series of recitatives conveying the action, interspersed with arias exploring various emotional states. It is Mozart's genius that makes these pieces so ravishing to the ear, so emotionally attuned to each human and dramatic situation and predicament, ending in *Idomeneo* in the triumph of love (Idamante is united with Ilia) and Idomeneo's self-sacrifice that wins the day over retributive justice. It was to conductor James Levine's credit that so much of the opera, in Daniel Heartz's modern edition, was performed (and so magisterially executed), including Elettra's three arias and Arbace's two. Only the final ballet was omitted because Ponnelle felt its very artificiality would ultimately detract from the dramatic building of human qualities he sought to bring out in the work. And Ponnelle could not restrain his enthusiasm at having Luciano Pavarotti in the title role (he had sung Idamante as a young tenor at the Glyndebourne Festival in the early 1960s): "At last I have an Italian singer in Mozart, which is difficult today! I prefer to have Italians when I have the chance because of the way they handle the language in the recitatives."

In performance, *Idomeneo* can seem like nothing more than a polite concert of splendid arias, a fossilized relic from the French *tragédie lyrique* tradition, but in Ponnelle's hands this is never allowed to happen. Each character is specifically delineated, not only in acting and in the costuming that gives an added dimension to each individual, but in the interaction between characters. Each dramatic action evolves rationally. From the very start, Ponnelle offers a striking triangle, as Idamante and Elettra claim their stage area during Ilia's initial recitative and aria, thus immediately establishing the amorous conflict in purely visual terms—almost as if these people are eavedropping on one another and keeping track of each other's most minute comings and goings. In Act II, Ilia (the captive Trojan princess) silently observes Elettra's gentle love aria, and for the act's finale Ponnelle boldly gathers his singers to encircle Idomeneo, closing in weblike on the guilty king whose action has caused Neptune to send a sea-monster and a fierce storm to afflict Crete. The plight of Idomeneo, faced with the prospect of having to sacrifice his son Idamante (he had agreed to sacrifice the first person he should meet after being saved from the sea), maintains pathos, while in Act III Agamemnon's daughter Elettra—played as a raving, vengeful, neurotic harridan from the start—is bent on magnificent self-destruction as she sings her aria "D'Oreste, d'Aiace," in which her inner seething finally boils over. Ponnelle has called Elettra "the greatest hysteric figure in opera," and he has her villainously stalking the stage in fiery red wig and outsized black hooped-skirt gown.

Behind all the action looms the mighty, menacing head of Neptune, the god whose actions have precipitated the dramatic conflict. Its stony classical presence can be felt throughout as it moves forward and recedes, like some gigantic tragic mask dominating the action and from whose cavelike mouth the Cretan king Idomeneo is initially spewn forth with his men after being shipwrecked on their return from the Trojan War. It remains a constant, striking emblem of the *numi implacabili* that rule human existence and hold Idomeneo to his vows. Commenting on this particular focal point, Ponnelle says, "I used the face of Neptune to express the father complex, because this is the key to the opera. Mozart finally found a way to be free himself from his own father's tyranny—I have great respect for his father, incidentally. We have Mozart's music because his father taught him. But Mozart eventually found his own personality, independent of his father's, when he worked on *Idomeneo*. Idamante, too, has a father complex, and Idomeneo a son complex. For Idomeneo, Neptune is the father he no longer has. He also exists as a guiding force in the lives of all these people."

As in his other productions, Ponnelle, listening to the dictates of the music, suavely blends classical and baroque styles to exceptional effect, contrasting the period of the action with the era in which the work was composed, counterbalancing poise with florid emotion run riot. Ponnelle's monochromatic color schemes tend to Renaissance sepia, beige, gray, and black, his pale scenic drops suggest Bibbiena or Piranesi, and his weathered-stone unit set represents a ruined Greek temple littered with crumbling, decayed, Ionic columns of the antique past as viewed through a Romantic filter. His costumes suggest the Grecian (especially for the Trojan princess Ilia, daughter of Priam) as well as the ornately rococo, occasionally spiced with rich purple for Idomeneo and his men who, in their white lacy jabots and curly wigs, somehow resemble members of the French Académie in their finery. With Gil Wechsler's dramatic lighting, colors are adroitly used not merely for picturesque effects, but to point up the dramatic

Act III. The High Priest (Timothy Jenkins) and the people of Crete outside the Temple of Neptune.

L'Italiana in Algeri

ROSSINI

Production: **Jean-Pierre Ponnelle**
Sets and Costumes: **Jean-Pierre Ponnelle**

action and enhance it. A single strong tone set against Ponnelle's essentially monochromatic color scheme makes for a striking theatrical effect.

Ponnelle also knows how to make the most expansive use of his chorus, whose members—in beige-and-white peasant dress (a constant image in many Ponnelle stagings of early operas)—became part of the stylized action, not just a neutral backdrop. The director-designer reasons that his idealized Romantic look at the classical past evolves out of the fact that in reality *Idomeneo* "is young Mozart, full of Romantic *Sturm und Drang*." Of his basic setting, with its classical columns, stone steps, and porticoes, he says that the characters have certain relationships in scenic space, like notes in the musical score, and that the staff lines are like steps onstage. "So I approach the problem from a graphic point of view. When the music goes up and down, my characters go up and down at the right time. The columns are eighteenth-century classical architecture with a nostalgia for antique architecture. So it all becomes a *nostalgie* for both the real antique past and the eighteenth century. It's neo-romantic and classical at the same time."

Ponnelle's characters, the creations of Mozart and his librettist Giovanni Battista Varesco, never stop merely to sing an aria and hold up the action. They seem part of a constantly ongoing action even in the most rigid set pieces, always revealing emotions on a large scale. He feels that Mozart, like Rossini, wrote two types of aria. The first has the action continuing right through the recitative-and-aria form, which presents no problem for stage action because the action is actually going on in the music. The second type of aria has music that reflects some kind of mood, so time no longer exists; such an aria is about being happy or sad or hungry or whatever, without any sense of real-life time (as in Ilia's "Zeffiretti lusinghieri"). "That represents the splendid abstraction and absurdity of opera," comments Ponnelle. "The musical structure of such an aria is important—that A-B-A form with its recapitulation. A director has to keep all this in mind and listen to the instruments in the accompaniment too. What is the horn or clarinet doing now? Does it wait, does it express what the character is expressing, or does it convey the character's real inner feelings at the moment? So the totality becomes a musical action which then has to be portrayed onstage.... In a work like *Idomeneo* you are having to operate at many different levels."

In a larger sense, one feels with *Idomeneo* that reason and human values triumph over the fateful demons of superstition, that the Age of Reason is what is celebrated in the opera's final moments. As Andrew Porter noted in *The New Yorker*, "The

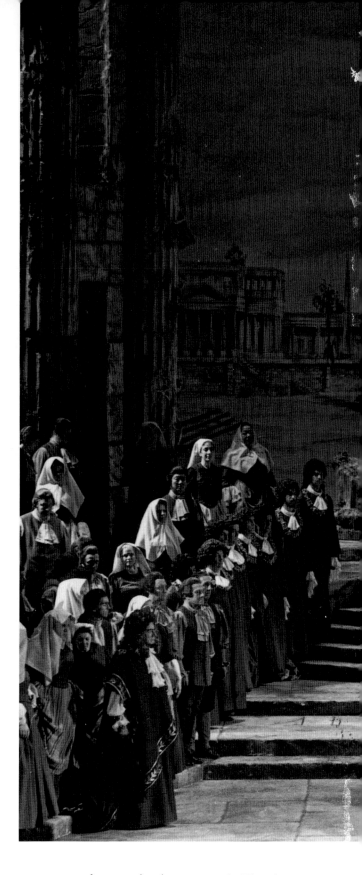

issues at stake are clearly presented. The drama moves powerfully. The style chosen combines directness and romance with due formality." Just as Mozart declared, "The audience must believe it is real," so Jean-Pierre Ponnelle makes this seemingly conventional and antiquated opera seria extraordinarily real and revealing in the theater.

Act III, Scene 3. The people of Crete gather outside the temple for the presentation of their new rulers, Idamante (Frederica Von Stade) and Ilia (Ileana Cotrubas), by Idomeneo (Luciano Pavarotti). At far left stands Arbace (John Alexander), and on the right the High Priest (Timothy Jenkins).

L'Italiana in Algeri

ROSSINI

Production: **Jean-Pierre Ponnelle**
Sets and Costumes: **Jean-Pierre Ponnelle**

L'Italiana in Algeri

IT WAS a Rossini comic delight, *L'Italiana in Algeri*, that first brought Jean-Pierre Ponnelle to the Metropolitan Opera as director-designer in November 1973, and he produced this opera again at La Scala several years later when Marilyn Horne re-created her incomparable Isabella, which had captivated New York. While brilliant in conception and execution, this production proved highly controversial with a New York press accustomed to the more traditional, more conventional, less sensual and freewheeling handling of opera buffa. *L'Italiana*, Rossini's tenth opera, composed in 1813 when he was only twenty-three, had not been heard at the Met since the 1919-20 season. The availability of the virtuoso talents of Marilyn Horne was the reason for its revival, and she was to interpret every aspect of Isabella's ebullient, commanding character and vocal agility in a manner that few others have succeeded in equaling—as well as proving herself to be a comedienne of the first order.

As with most of his productions, Ponnelle conceived it within the bounds of one of his chief trademarks: a sophisticated, muted color scheme, against which the introduction of one strong color at a particularly theatrical moment makes a powerful statement. Here, in order to convey the feeling of the North African desert, he chose a glowing beige color, suggestive of sandstone, which dominated his arabesque-filled, permanent, box-shaped setting of arches, steps, and ramps of the Bey's Moorish palace. Curtains, latticed screens, movable palm trees, and other props helped to alter locales for the various scenes within the palace.

Above and opposite, top
Costume designs by Jean-Pierre Ponnelle for Mustafà, Bey of Algiers, and for his wife Elvira and her slave Zulma.

◁ *Overleaf*
The eunuchs who guard the harem in the Bey's palace in Algiers (*inset*), and one of their prisoners, Isabella (Marilyn Horne), in Turkish attire during her aria "Per lui che adoro."

Looking back on his designing career, Ponnelle relates, "I began by using too much color. Eventually I found that monochrome and variations are more satisfactory for the stage. Then one contrasting color becomes much stronger than presenting many colors all at once. Of course, using a monochrome depends on the piece at hand, but I like the subtlety, say, of using two different grays rather than white and blue. In painters I prefer Braque and Gris to Matisse, or Velázquez to Titian. So when you use a bright color, it really means something! Onstage everything is a symbol. Color takes on dramaturgical significance. It's like a tonality for a composer in this aria or that—it all has its meaning. If you put red or green here and there, it may be fine as a painting but *not* for the stage. I use color to enhance the drama of the piece."

So it is with *L'Italiana in Algeri*, with its warm tones conveying the mood of a hot, dry country. Since Isabella, the Italian girl of the title, and Mustafà, the Bey of Algiers, are the protagonists, their costumes feature the strongest colors, while the other characters wear various gradations of white, beige, and brown in relation to their theatrical importance. Isabella's companion Taddeo, for instance, is attired in drab, conservative dress, as befits his stuffy personality, while the Bey's wife Elvira appears in sparkling white. Lindoro, the spirited, moonstruck Italian in love with Isabella, but a captured slave of the Bey, sports a natty double-breasted, navy-blue blazer with gold buttons, like the captain of some luxury yacht. The self-possessed Isabella is first seen coming ashore from her wrecked ship in a splendid Black Watch tartan traveling suit, complete with white gloves, snappy straw hat with flowers, and carrying a parasol, ready for her "Cruda sorte" declarations to her captors. Later, she appears in a dazzling black-and-white gown, complemented by a tall feathered headdress and an outsized feathery fan, primed to make her outrageous asides of "Oh! che muso, che figura! . . . quali occhiate" when she meets the Bey at his court and can barely restrain her mocking contempt. (This striking figure in the midst of pale-colored surroundings is not unlike Cinderella's appearance at the prince's ball in Rossini's *La Cenerentola*, a work that Ponnelle has directed at La Scala, in San Francisco, and for television.) For Isabella's lovely, *grazioso* "Per lui che adoro," sung as she prepares herself for Mustafà in her boudoir, she positively glows in a shocking-pink confection with matching turban in the Turkish style. Mustafà, desiring a European woman to displace his spouse (with whom he is now bored), greets her in spectacular black-and-white finery, thus in Ponnelle's eyes making them worthy adversaries in the duel of the sexes. The chorus of palace eunuchs are done up in uniform false faces and protruding bellies, as they sew in unison in the Bey's harem. Ponnelle sought a kind of stylized mass here, something abstract and without individual faces, more "a block, a cliché." "But," he adds, "when Isabella sings of Italian political matters in 'Pensa alla patria,' the members of the chorus become individual Italian men, recognizable people. So the reality depends on the music." He feels that *L'Italiana in Algeri* is not an easy work to bring to life onstage, as opposed to *Il Barbiere di Siviglia*, which is a more realistic comedy. *La Cenerentola* is unrealistic too, with characters who are not always easy to understand.

Above and right

Act I. Wrapped in a towel after a steam bath, Mustafà (Fernando Corena), attended by Elvira (Christine Weidinger) and the pirate chief Haly (Gene Boucher), relishes the prospect of making a new conquest—the shipwrecked Isabella; and Lindoro (Luigi Alva) tells the unwilling Elvira that she should leave her husband.

Act I. Mustafà (Fernando Corena) awaits his first encounter with the shipwrecked Isabella (*opposite*). The Italian girl (Marilyn Horne) makes her entrance (*right*) with the bravura aria "Cruda sorte."

Below
Act II. Mustafà (Fernando Corena) is made to believe he is being inducted into the Italian order of "Pappataci"; Lindoro (Luigi Alva) and Taddeo (Theodor Uppman), both planning to escape, play the trick on the gullible Bey.

Overall, Ponnelle has sought to create a delicious comedy of manners amid two contrasting worlds—the seemingly fiercer Eastern one of the Bey and the more civilized West of the cunning Isabella. This is the domain of opera buffa, and to Ponnelle's mind these characters celebrate its glories all the while they are making gentle fun of it and of its conventions. Ponnelle sees comedy as just a slight extension of reality, and his characters, while often buffo stereotypes, take on very human qualities, foibles and all; they ultimately prove to be hilariously entertaining, as well as warm and touching. Ponnelle stops just short of real burlesque, reinforcing Rossini's musical caricature and achieving a delicate balance of true wit. The one questionable decision was to set Act I, Scene 3 (with Mustafà's "Già d'insolito ardore nel petto"), in the Bey's tiled steam bath, the Bey himself being—apparently—wrapped only in a large white towel as he makes his exit.

Still, Ponnelle's nonstop stage devices are totally captivating, beginning with the hilarious shipwreck of Act I, Scene 2: the ignited cannon aimed by the Bey's men (who have been ordered to find a European woman for the bored Bey) sinks a tiny toy ship on the horizon, and from this Isabella and her retinue appear, neat and orderly, ready to be conducted to Mustafà, with Isabella ever prepared to take matters into her own hands. At the palace, when Isabella and Mustafà finally confront one another, sliding ramps move them in and out of prominence and focus during the ensembles, all brilliantly timed to the music and their respective roles in it. Ponnelle's individualizing of all the principals in the hilarious Act I ensemble—with their heads ringing like bells or beating like hammers, Taddeo crowing and Mustafà's head roaring like a cannon, all set to an accompaniment of "din-din," "tac-tac," "cra-cra," "bum-bum," etc.—was an inspired touch, used to side-splitting effect as each character seems to be going mad in his or her own separate world. In the final plot of investing Mustafà with the honorary title of "Pappataci," he must only eat, drink, and keep quiet, and here Ponnelle has Isabella prepare and feed him her own special spaghetti, which the Bey busily winds on his fork, rapt in concentration, as Isabella and Lindoro prepare to make their escape by boat.

All these comic effects are accomplished with the utmost wit and style, revitalizing a work that could in less capable hands seem an empty farce, and are achieved with the aid of every modern theatrical device, a rousing sense of humor, and an almost nonstop battery of visual ideas, all combining to underline Rossini's scintillating score. With *L'Italiana in Algeri*, Rossini reached the full flower of his youth, and Ponnelle matches the composer's wit, elegance, polish, and panache. One might have agreed with the critic Stendhal's observation at the Venice premiere of the opera: ". . . musical Venice, rating lightness of heart above depth of passion, looks first and foremost for songs that entrance the ear. In *L'Italiana* the prayers of the people of Venice were abundantly granted; no race ever witnessed an entertainment better suited to its own character; and of all the operas ever composed, none was more truly destined to be the joy and delight of Venice." In Ponnelle's deft hands it was to become—over a century-and-a-half later—a joy and delight to New York audiences as well.

Lulu

BERG

Production: **John Dexter**
Sets and Costumes: **Jocelyn Herbert**
Lighting: **Gil Wechsler**

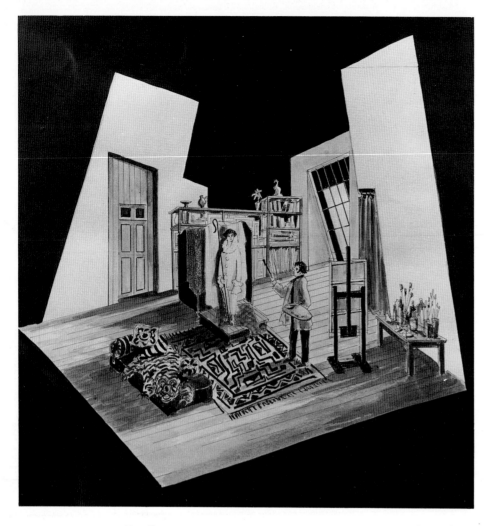

Lulu

ALBAN BERG'S two operas, *Lulu* and *Wozzeck*, have come to be regarded as twentieth-century masterpieces. Rudolf Bing dared to introduce *Wozzeck* into the Met repertory back in 1959, but it took nearly forty years for the original (incomplete) version of *Lulu* to arrive at the Met after its Zurich world premiere in 1937. It had meanwhile been staged in most of the world's leading opera houses, and was hailed as a musico-dramatic experience of rare fascination and brilliance. This strange, expressionistic story, with its deep symbolism and decadent ambience, is a litany of sex, death, murder, suicide, and morbid obsessions, reeking of 1920s daring and Freudian revelations. It runs the risk of appearing naive, even ludicrous, in the more sexually open world of today. Yet part of *Lulu*'s undeniable power lies in the multi-layered meanings and interpretations with which it is invested, first through the two plays by Frank Wedekind—*Earth Spirit* and *Pandora's Box*—that inspired the opera, then through Berg's terse, chilling adaptation of the material. The composer's dense, concentrated scoring not only provides a mesmeric sense of drama, but portrays each of the main characters with uncommon force. Wedekind turned against the tradition of natura-

Above

Design by Jocelyn Herbert for Act I, Scene 1.

Right

Prologue. Lulu (Teresa Stratas), in Pierrot costume, is borne in by a circus hand to be introduced to the audience by the Ringmaster (Lenus Carlson).

◁ *Overleaf*

Act II, Scene 1. After a heated argument, Lulu (Teresa Stratas) murders her husband Dr. Schön (Franz Mazura).

lism in the theater, creating episodic images derived from the tradition of circuses, cabarets, vaudeville, and pantomime. His are moral allegories that are bedecked in theatricality and spectacle. In the theater, his series of grotesque caricatures, who do not always develop psychologically or even coherently, reflect back to the audience a true image of itself—in much the same way as the incisive, brutal drawings of George Grosz had done somewhat earlier in the century.

When, in 1977, James Levine conducted its incomplete but eloquent house premiere of *Lulu*, the Met did rather more than most stagings elsewhere had attempted up to that time. At his death in 1935, Berg left his third act unfinished, and until her death in 1976 his widow, Helene, adamantly refused to allow it to be completed, although most of the material existed, awaiting editing and final orchestration. Director John Dexter staged the first two acts just as Berg conceived them, and accomplished the third by using the Variations and Adagio of the *Lulu* Suite plus the Ostinato, with spoken dialogue, pantomime, and slides, as had customarily been done. But he then added a small scene from *Pandora's Box*, showing Lulu and her demimonde friends at a Paris gambling casino, in which she was thrust forcibly into whoredom by the Marquis (presaging that scene in the eventually completed version). Dexter conceived the psychological drama in a straight, clear manner, uncluttered, precise, and

tight, thus achieving a highly naturalistic course of action in which male society forces degradation on women. Yet Dexter's style deliberately played against the expressionistic slant of the original. This staging could easily have worked as a straight play; there was no sign of old-fashioned operatic gesture as the performance mixed tragedy and violence with the intentional farce and crudity of the sources. With such operas as *Lulu*, Poulenc's *Dialogues des Carmélites*, and Britten's *Billy Budd*, Dexter was not only inspired to some of his most successful work at the Met, but helped to expand the theater's repertory to include modern operas. He commented, "I want to open the door wider on the twentieth century, keep an eye on something more than survival into the future—make a gesture for the future. The sweetening on the pill is to give audiences modern music while doing a *presentation*. In each case you must be visually simple while having a theatrical concept."

It was this theory that brought Berg's *Lulu* into such strong focus. Jocelyn Herbert's evocative *fin-de-siècle* decor reveled in pre-World War I period detail, her small, flexible, fragmented unit sets coming and going smoothly and quickly. These ranged from the Art Nouveau of Lulu's home, to the Bauhaus style and Art Deco of Lulu's theater dressing room (where she coolly demands that Dr. Schön give up his fiancée and marry her, thereby precipitating his ruin), to the heavy, baronial splendor of Dr. Schön's respectable residence with its twisted wooden columns and plush furniture (where she shoots her husband and later, at the end of Act II, consummates her affair with his son Alwa on the couch where his father died). Here, Herbert splendidly contrasts the girl's decadent, amoral world with the man's bourgeois position of power, status, money, and security. Finally, in Act III, there is the sparse, cold London attic, a dirty and derelict place in which Lulu (by now forced into prostitution) and her ever-faithful lesbian admirer, the Countess Geschwitz, die so sordidly by Jack the Ripper's slashing knife as the drama reaches its grisly climax.

Above

Act I, Scene 1. In the studio of the Painter (Frank Little, behind easel), Dr. Schön (Franz Mazura) and the composer Alwa (Kenneth Riegel) stand before the portrait of Lulu (Teresa Stratas) as she holds her pose.

Overleaf ▷

Act I, Scene 3. Lulu (Teresa Stratas), now a dancer, strikes a dramatic pose in her theater dressing room (*right*), where she forces Dr. Schön (Franz Mazura) to write a letter (*left*) renouncing his fiancée.

Lulu 135

When, in December 1980, the Met turned to Berg's *Lulu* once again, much about its history and structure had been significantly altered. The score had been completed by the Austrian composer and conductor Friedrich Cerha, and this version had had its world premiere at the Paris Opéra in February 1979, followed by its U.S. premiere at the Santa Fe Opera that summer. The realization of *Lulu* after all these years proved to be one of the major musical and operatic events in the years since the end of World War II. Cerha's use of Berg's existing—but previously suppressed—materials and of his formal plan for Act III seems completely in step with the composer's overall view, and the final scene in particular develops the once unresolved relationships of Lulu, Geschwitz, Alwa, and Schigolch—a quartet chilling in its emotional interplay.

Below

Act I, Scene 2. Lulu (Carole Farley) in the Painter's drawing room with Alwa (William Lewis) and Dr. Schön (Donald Gramm).

Dexter's 1977 version had prepared the way for the Met to undertake the full edition, and the company proceeded to turn it into an emotionally galvanizing experience. With Teresa Stratas now in the title role and with Franz Mazura as Dr. Schön (the roles had previously been sung by Carole Farley and Donald Gramm), the director fell heir to two veterans of the Paris staging by the French *enfant terrible*, Patrice Chéreau. Their

adversarial scenes possessed a frightening intensity. Stratas portrayed Lulu as a feline, earthy, disturbing creature, truly a child of nature—a deadly innocent caught up in a stream of sexual action and reaction. Although her actions are in no way premeditated, she is nevertheless a predator by nature. Lulu exists as a passive victim of male importunity; she remains indifferent to her victims, while refusing the pigeon-holes to which men assign her. In her dissolute innocence, Lulu is uniquely and devastatingly honest—hers is a candor that kills. And that very honesty terrorizes a society filled with evasion, false morality and double standards. Lulu's tragedy is that she finally falls victim to the system, and it destroys her. In her powerful portrayal, Stratas encompassed all Lulu's prismatic qualities with remarkable subtlety, as she alternated between wide-eyed innocence and veiled anger. Confident in her sexuality, she remained strangely beautiful even when returning home after her life-sapping term in prison, gray and wasted by cholera, but ever the true *Erdgeist*. As Stratas has said of the role, "People see only what they want to see in Lulu. But she's not just black and white: she is the total spectrum of colors and personalities."

Above
Act II, Scene 2. Following her escape from the prison hospital, Lulu (Teresa Stratas) seeks protection from Alwa (Kenneth Riegel).

Lulu   139

Above

Act III, Scene 2. In a London garret, Geschwitz (Evelyn Lear) embraces the portrait depicting her beloved Lulu in Pierrot costume.

Left

Act III, Scene 1. Lulu (Teresa Stratas) and a member of her ménage, the elderly Schigolch (Andrew Foldi), hatch a plan to get rid of Rodrigo, the troublesome athlete.

Top

Act III, Scene 1. Lulu (Teresa Stratas) persuades Geschwitz (Evelyn Lear) to submit to the unwanted attentions of the blackmailing Rodrigo in order to save her from being denounced to the police.

Right

Director John Dexter rehearsing Act I with Carole Farley, who sang the title role in 1977, and Donald Gramm, the original Dr. Schön.

Opposite

Act III, Scene 2. On the run and forced into prostitution, Lulu (Teresa Stratas) is seen in the London garret with her final client, Jack the Ripper (Franz Mazura), who haggles with her before she becomes yet another of his victims.

Mazura's big, hawklike presence, combined with his forceful acting skills, riveted the audience's attention as he first explored Dr. Schön's complex blend of cruelty, despair, and love, acting out a moral collapse that was appalling to witness—then returned in his sinister portrayal of the bowler-hatted Jack the Ripper. Interestingly, Dexter follows Berg's view of *Lulu* as a modern morality play: the singer playing the publishing tycoon Schön, who is killed by Lulu in self-defense, should then play the legendary killer, Jack the Ripper, who in turn murders Lulu at the end. Lulu ascends the social ladder until she kills Schön, after which progressive degradation sets in. The femme fatale unintentionally destroys everyone who comes in contact with her, and so she herself is destroyed by the alter egos of her three husbands in the final scene of Act III. (In a dramatic parallel, Lulu's former husbands, the Physician and the Painter of Act I, return in Act III in the guise of the prostitute's clients.) These people become allies in a round of mutual destruction.

Each of the bizarre characters in *Lulu* is brought graphically to life: the mannish, patrician, selfless Geschwitz; the strange, dirty old man, Schigolch; Rodrigo, the strutting, lustful athlete; the innocent Schoolboy; and so on. Without reverting to any sensationalism, Dexter's modern, theatrical ensemble direction is vividly cohesive and purposeful in delineating all the complex, sometimes vague, relationships, while generally remaining faithful to Berg's intention. The director and designer weave the crucial thread of continuity with the image of Lulu as Pierrot. During the Prologue, she is introduced in Pierrot costume by the Ringmaster as the root of all evil, a snake created to cause grief and pain, to lure and seduce and fill with venom. Lulu is then being painted as Pierrot during Scene 1, and that portrait (a symbolic reminder of Lulu as she was before her rise and fall) travels everywhere with her until, at the end of Act III, Geschwitz dies stranded between the murdered Lulu and her Pierrot idealization, as she calls out Lulu's name.

Jocelyn Herbert's varied wardrobe captures Lulu's many moods and situations, and her sets are not only consistent, visually varied, and always interesting in their detail, but provide well-focused playing areas that seem to thrust the action right into the audience's lap. Her hard-edged Paris casino is filled with green baize gaming tables and mirrored surfaces, reflecting the audience back to itself, much as Berg's own opera and Wedekind's plays do so frighteningly. As Berg himself observed, "Only through an understanding of the sensual through a profound insight into the depth—or perhaps the heights—of mankind can one arrive at a true idea of the human psyche."

Manon Lescaut

PUCCINI

Production: **Gian Carlo Menotti**
Sets and Costumes: **Desmond Heeley**   Lighting: **Gil Wechsler**

Manon Lescaut

ONE recent trend in production style at the Met has been a preference for the traditional, realisitic approach. Certainly in standard repertory pieces, the feeling has been that sturdy, naturalistic, uncontroversial stagings will have a longer life in the repertory than the trendy ones, which soon become outdated and difficult to maintain. One of the most applauded efforts in this respect was the sumptuous 1980 production of *Manon Lescaut*, directed by Gian Carlo Menotti and designed by Desmond Heeley; this was the Met's first new staging, since the memorable 1949 version with Dorothy Kirsten and Jussi Bjoerling, of what had been Puccini's initial great success. Menotti, a guest director both in the United States and elsewhere with his own operas as well as a wide repertory of others, had not applied his directorial touch at the Met since his own *The Last Savage* received its American premiere in 1964.

When the curtain rose on the lavish set depicting the weathered stagecoach-stop in Amiens, the communal fountain, a massive wooden gate, leafy trees, and a deep-hued sky, all supplemented with a real horse and carriage for the arrival of the convent-bound Manon, one knew this was to be an evening of old-style flamboyance. Desmond Heeley's costumes evoked rugged country garb and the subdued colors of a Chardin painting as contrasted with the exquisite subtlety of a Watteau. As with his own works for the stage (which often seem like latter-day extensions of Italian *verismo*) and his other lyric theater stagings, Menotti sought a highly detailed realism to bring off the opera's four loosely connected tableaux culled from the Abbé Prévost novel and adapted by Puccini's team of librettists. Menotti desired something charming and lovely in the visual sense,

to which he added direction of the most human, characterful persuasion. Director and designer seemed in total accord in seeking to provide a handsome show that would fill the stage but never to the point of overwhelming its inhabitants, and at the same time to convey a true sense of time and place. The principal characters were kept front and center, well focused, so that their background never completely absorbed them or deflected the audience's attention; and Menotti never seemed embarrassed by the effusion of emotions from the two lovers, which one critic in Puccini's time called "the impetuous artistic vigor of youth."

Desmond Heeley, who takes the sane route of looking after all the practical necessities of a production before thinking about the decorative embellishments, says he "wanted to create the *illusion* of reality, because realism in itself becomes dull. So it's a kind of heightened realism, such as the Act II boudoir which extends and heightens architectural and decorative realism. It's like the eye of the camera, in which the depth of field is used to center in on the performer, while leaving the rest a bit fuzzy around the edges.

"I also feel," he adds, "that the first ten feet from the curtain line is the most important space, because that's where all the action happens. And it keeps the singers and conductors happy because down there they can see one another and communicate."

Basically, Heeley sought to show that an eighteenth-century setting can be beautiful and strong, not just pretty: "It's not the Hollywood of white wigs and satin bows. It's not dainty, but strong and masculine like the Amalienburg Palace." He felt that his initial concept was not fully realized—particularly in Act IV where he had wanted a black, desolate sky and steep hills with deep ridges of sand so that attention would be completely focused on Manon and Des Grieux. He sought to move from an Italianate, sun-drenched atmosphere in Act I to a more coolly formal townhouse interior in Act II, then the chilling reality of impending deportation from Le Havre in Act III, and finally the bleak, desolate New World atmosphere of Act IV; but the last was rendered somewhat more romantic by the use of the red sky drop from Act I. Throughout, Heeley felt that the eighteenth century was being viewed through the eyes of the nineteenth century to achieve what he insists is "the illusion of reality."

A rich slice of life is at hand in Act I, with its rambling, two-storied inn, the spill of tables and benches in the stone courtyard, bathed in browns and reds, the progress from hot afternoon to warm evening, complete with candles for the tables and ongoing card games. Vendors, students, villagers, children bustle about and play, while women of

Above

Renata Scotto, who sang the title role in 1980, in conversation with director Gian Carlo Menotti.

◁ *Overleaf*

Act IV. The dying Manon (Mirella Freni) despairs in the New World—"Sola, perduta, abbandonata."

Act III (*inset*). The faithful Des Grieux (Placido Domingo) pleads with the ship's Captain (Russell Christopher) to be allowed to sail to America with Manon— "No! pazzo son! guardate!"

questionable virtue roll down their colored stockings, busily wash their feet, and tread grapes. The luggage-laden coach makes a spectacular entry through the Paris Gate at stage rear to deposit its various passengers, including the shy, reticent Manon, traveling to Amiens with her sergeant brother, Lescaut. At this crossroads of French society, Manon and Des Grieux meet and immediately fall in love. When, in the midst of much drinking and gambling, the couple escape into the night to catch Geronte's prearranged coach, their departure takes place offstage, since the arrival coach remains onstage.

In Prévost's story and in Massenet's *Manon*, the couple live together modestly in Paris, but in Puccini's opera we jump immediately to the girl's privileged ensconcement in Geronte's opulent Paris home, where, as befits the mistress of an important Treasury official, she lives in the height of luxury. Heeley designed a gaudy, ornate boudoir, heavy and almost oppressive in its rococo detail—much as Manon finds her life confining, as expressed in the aria "In quelle trine morbide." The tarnished mirrored columns, the silvery green coloration, pewtery walls, heavy velvet swags, and glittering chandeliers are spectacular and decadent in their visual impact, but at the same time parody Geronte's ostentation and his luxurious taste, as well as his extravagant spoiling of Manon. To the right is Manon's dressing table, to the left an enormous unmade bed, which serves as the location for the passionate Manon–Des Grieux love duet; and it is on that bed that they are interrupted by Geronte. Some years back, at the Spoleto Festival, Luchino Visconti too conceived Act II of *Manon Lescaut* in terms of such blatant sensuality, the key to which lies in the erotic outpourings of the duet. Manon's frilly white gown contrasts superbly with the exotically garbed and plumed musicians in their reds and oranges, as it does with the severe black of the primping, bewigged abbés and rich gentlemen, to whom the overly elegant, foppish Geronte shows Manon off as his latest prize during the levée scene. Heeley wanted a showy room in which color is played down, in order to bring the characters into relief. The scattered pillows and the bed in disorder serve to contrast with the conventional idea of the orderliness of the eighteenth century, a period which, notes Heeley, "was actually enormously sensual."

Act I. After alighting from the coach at Amiens, Manon (Renata Scotto) is seen with her brother Lescaut (Pablo Elvira) and their fellow passenger, Geronte (Renato Capecchi); Manon's charms have already attracted the attention of Des Grieux (Placido Domingo, center foreground) and his young friend Edmondo (Philip Creech).

Act II. Set design by Desmond Heeley for Manon's Paris bedroom, where (*above*) the heroine (Mirella Freni) primps at her dressing table and later amuses her Dancing Master (Andrea Velis) and her elderly patron Geronte (Ara Berberian).

Act III. Des Grieux (Placido Domingo) comes to visit Manon (Renata Scotto), imprisoned at Le Havre.

Act III again offers a sense of real place and time at the bleak quayside of Le Havre, where Manon awaits deportation to America. Leaving an impressive, fluid playing area stage center for the town observers and roll call of French prostitutes who are being sent to the New World, Heeley places the gangplank, masted ship, and heavy-timbered wharf at an angle to the right, with the prison house far left, all in a tight, forward-pushing impression of wall, steps, and prison bars. The rough-hewn character of the northern French seaport is expertly crafted, all set against the menacing gray of an early-morning sky.

The final act always poses problems for a designer, for its setting is meant to be a vast "desert plain on the borders of New Orleans," where Manon and her lover have been deposited in France's North American territory. Puccini and his writers knew little of American geography, the actual Louisiana location being more bayou than desert. Against a dramatic crimson sky, Heeley designed two mounded levels of arid, almost abstract or stylized desert in which the lovers could spend their final moments together. A skeleton of some animal, picked clean by vultures, lies off to one side as evidence of the impossibility of survival in this desolate wilderness, where Manon will find her final resting place. Windswept starkness, arid bleakness, hopelessness are all superbly conveyed in this realistic yet symbolic final picture, providing—in its primeval vastness—a total contrast to the precious civilization of eigthteenth-century France.

Menotti's shrewdly simple direction went hand in glove with these designs. There was little deviation from past *Manon Lescaut* stagings, but his keen eye for character detail added up to full-blooded portrayals, together with a splendid sense of humorous cynicism. Manon enters as the shy, innocent teenager, eager to participate in the teeming activity all around her at Amiens. Her attraction to Des Grieux is as immediate as his is to her, and the ardent, youthful pair instantly become absorbed in their own carefree, amorous world as they chase off to Paris. Menotti paints the young man with great depth too—as Prévost's true *homme sensible*, a man of feeling for whom ecstasy is superior to reason, who embodies the conflict between feeling and duty, and who reveals his allegiance to "passion in its pure state." In fact, it is the young man's insistent temptations which pave the way for the girl's downfall, and he remains an ambiguous figure, mixing virtue and vice, "a perpetual contrast of good sentiments and bad actions," as Prévost described him. Manon's brother Lescaut has all the necessary bravado and self-centeredness, a man taking on the responsibility of looking after his sister but infinitely more interested in cards, drinking, and money. Geronte is played with just the right amount of ennui as well as lechery, remaining above those around him— save for the simple peasant girl Manon.

The Manon of Act II proves to be greatly altered. While enlisting sympathy in her first scene with the visiting Lescaut, she then reveals herself as a pouting, spoiled, self-preoccupied minx with an inordinate attachment to the jewelry heaped on her—the very embodiment of materialism. For this young country girl, suddenly exposed to Parisian high life, the refinements of the musicians are merely boring, as they are for Lescaut, who, on making his entrance, casually tosses his hat on a chair, and who exhibits throughout the act his own brand of insouciant confidence and boorishness. Barely tolerating the Dancing Master (how much she prefers her hairdressers!), Manon, having lost one of her brilliant earrings to complete her afternoon ensemble, searches for it furiously during the madrigal, coming up with it amid the pile of pillows on the unmade bed. But Menotti's emphasis on her exaggerated attachment to jewelry turns some of the action into unintentional comedy in the manner of Feydeau. Ultimately, making Manon appear so tough, so petulant, so basically unpleasant and even cruel, tends to drain whatever sympathy one might muster for her—and this runs counter to Puccini's own conception of his heroines, who tend to elicit almost an excess of sympathy. The amoral Manon's longing for more sensual pleasures and excitement—frustrated in this formal environment and her loveless relationship with Geronte—explodes in the love duet with Des Grieux and its passionate climax on the bed.

Then in the haste of trying to escape Geronte's revenge, after Manon has showed him his own aged reflection in the mirror, the girl gathers up whatever valuables she can lay her hands on, wraps them in a shawl, only to have them dramatically fall from her trembling hands, spilling and scattering across the floor as the police arrest her and drag her off to prison.

Manon' disgrace is immediately evident in Act III, her fine white gown now dirty and tattered as she has been tossed in with the lowest of France's low life, a prisoner of her own greed and selfishness as much as of the state. She is already a broken spirit, a young girl whose quest for *la dolce vita* has brought her to this mean iron cage on the quayside at Le Havre. Des Grieux remains loyal to his temptress, hoping to secure her freedom but then begging to be allowed to sail with her so that they can live together in the New World. As the name of each prostitute is called by the Sergeant, the various individuals exhibit—each in her own way—flirtatiousness, resignation, coquetry, arrogance, and even tragedy, while Manon remains defeated, sad, a broken bird. But she and Des Grieux are ecstatically reunited on board ship once the Captain has been moved by Des Grieux's desperate plea.

Finally, on the plains of Louisiana, the pair trudge across the sands, alone and abandoned. The heroine's health and spirits have been completely broken, her will to live falters as the sun sets on this vast wasteland. In Manon's lengthy death scene, a sense of intimacy, vulnerability, and touching power is maintained as the girl cowers, panting for water, a frail waif whose life is slowly ebbing away. With the exceptional artistry of a Renata Scotto or a Mirella Freni, and their meticulous care in the coloration of words, phrases, and mood, this scene evolves into one of potent tragedy, despite Manon's previous flightiness, heartlessness, and materialism. And Des Grieux's helplessness and despair become equally moving, for one senses that the man would have done anything in his power to restore Manon's life to her, and in the fashion she so desired.

As Thor Eckert, Jr., so aptly noted in the *Christian Science Monitor*, this lively, idiomatic, picturesque *Manon Lescaut* "heralds the return of old-fashioned values in operatic stagings, and is proof again that the best opera production is one wherein the composer's wishes are meticulously respected, one which does not hamper the singers, and does not succumb to the distortions of a director's concept."

Act IV. The distraught Des Grieux (Placido Domingo) weeps over the body of Manon (Renata Scotto).

Otello

VERDI

Production: **Franco Zeffirelli**   Sets: **Franco Zeffirelli**
Costumes: **Peter J. Hall**

Otello

THE massive solidity of the flourishing, civilized European world versus the terrifying instability and savagery of the Moor—this seemed to be what Franco Zeffirelli, as director and designer, was attempting to portray in his first production of Verdi's *Otello*, created for the Metropolitan Opera in 1972. In fact, he provided the audience with as much to think about as to experience visually and theatrically. The very grandeur and pomp of this production—it was called a "super-spectacular" by one critic—also marked Rudolf Bing's final bequest to the institution he had managed for the past twenty-two years, for it was the last such project planned by him before his retirement in the spring of 1972. And what a final bequest it was to prove! For aside from a controversial, hotly debated last act, Zeffirelli reaches into the heart of Shakespeare's tragedy, as adapted by Arrigo Boito and Giuseppe Verdi, in a style of intense realism that occasionally steps into the realm of melodrama. This is especially true of his ideas about the title role: Otello is portrayed as a man with a paranoid sense of insecurity, subject to mercurial changes in temper. As a result, his tragic flaw lies not in mere jealousy, the outcome of overwhelming blind passion, but in pathetic insanity.

Symbolically, Zeffirelli's designs move from the wide-open expanses of sea and sky in Act I to ever-increasing darkness and interior suffocation, ending in Act IV with an almost crypt-like bedroom for Desdemona, where the crazed Moor comes to seek his revenge for her supposed infidelity and smothers her to death. Thus, the openness, honesty, and embracing of nature that are the essence of Act I at the Cyprus seaport, where Otello and his crew navigate to shore at the height

of a violent storm, provide a strong contrast to the closed-off chamber of Desdemona, where reason and clarity of mind cannot possibly thrive. Massive Gothic stone towers silently stand guard throughout the opera, like the cultivated European consciousness silently looking down and brooding on the growing madness of the savage protagonist, the heroic man of war who has taken his Venetian bride to the crossroads of civilization and barbarism in Cyprus. As Zeffirelli has said of his approach to the theater: "An audience must never be allowed to lose the first impression that moves them." And the spectacular storm he has created to open the opera stays in the mind as a portent of the personal emotional storms to be played out in the course of the four acts.

Zeffirelli conceived a highly dramatic, taut *Otello* with detail after detail brilliantly thought through, then realized onstage, beginning with this realistic storm of gale-force winds, thunder, and flashes of lightning, and the arrival of Otello's ship in port, accompanied by the tempestuous rolling of waves, seaspray at the dock, and the swaying masts of several moored ships. One can almost smell the salt water and feel the spray being tossed onto the rocks. Otello delivers his "Esultate," celebrating the defeat of the Turkish fleet, from the high deck of the rescued galleon before he comes down to the port, then mounts the broad stone steps that lead to the castle and his waiting wife. Stormy darkness quickly turns to warmth of improvised fires in the port, a congenial atmosphere in which Iago (Jago), previously passed over by Otello when he promoted Cassio to lieutenant, can work his plot against the commanding Moor. Getting Cassio drunk on wine, he incites him to a fight, thus provoking the reappearance of Otello, who demotes the young soldier. When the crowds have dispersed, Otello and his radiant Desdemona are seen alone on the quay with the boats now peacefully rocking in harbor, the moon and stars aglow in the sky. They sing their exquisite love music in an atmosphere of peace and stillness, declaring their mutual love before slowly returning to the castle. Shakespeare never seems far away, for in his costume designs Peter J. Hall puts the emphasis on Elizabethan theater styles, with Desdemona in the high collar and great silken skirt and cloak of that period, and Otello in voluminous red and gold capes.

Zeffirelli's thoroughness in handling both emotional and physical detail is clearly demonstrated in Act II, in which he has Otello, as governor of Cyprus, temporarily established in a courtyard of the medieval fortress, his desk and books and maps housed under hastily improvised canvas shelters set up as protection against the elements, particularly the glare of the Mediterranean sun. Desdemona

Above
Director Franco Zeffirelli rehearsing Act II with Sherrill Milnes, the first Iago in 1972

◁ *Overleaf*
Act III, Scene 1. Otello (James McCracken) jealously demands the return of the handkerchief he gave Desdemona (Teresa Zylis-Gara) during their courtship.

promenades not in the traditional setting of a garden, but on the partially revealed ramparts, where the ladies and children of the castle are singing her praises. To emphasize and reinforce Iago's place with Otello, Zeffirelli chose to make him responsible for the books and papers. He was criticized for making the villain into an Elizabethan librarian, but what comes through most strongly is Otello's vast knowledge of European history and warfare, attained with Iago's help, and his reliance on this diabolically clever man who is destined to be his undoing. Iago can only work on Otello's mind if the latter has given him full trust, and this is wonderfully revealed in the scene during which Cassio can be observed with Desdemona, pleading his case in the hope that she will intercede with Otello on his behalf. The ease with which Otello can be manipulated by Iago is clearly

portrayed, ending in the fierce "Ora per sempre," in which Otello's call for vengeance is conveyed with manic desperation. Earlier, Iago's revelatory "Credo" ends not with sardonic laughter but with him cringing and creeping offstage in silent terror, as if fearing divine retribution.

Some thirteen years later, baritone Sherrill Milnes recalls the controversy of this moment: "I objected to Zeffirelli's convention of no open laughter, as is usually done. Iago was to feel some exorcist force inside himself, so he screamed and grabbed his head—but he didn't laugh mockingly. I never felt this, but I tried, and I got killed in the reviews. Still, we're dealing with a genius with Franco. In rehearsing you have to do what he means, not always what he says. You have to have a dialogue with him and question, and not be a puppet."

Act I. On the dock, outside the castle, Otello (Jon Vickers) and Desdemona (Teresa Zylis-Gara) recall the first days of their love.

Act II. Iago (Sherrill Milnes),
unpacking Otello's maps and
books, voices his bitter
denunciation—"Credo."
(*Above*) Desdemona (Teresa
Zylis-Gara) and her attendant
Emilia (Shirley Love) with a
group of admiring Cypriots
bringing gifts.

Otello's gullible nature is further explored in Act III, Scene 1, set by Zeffirelli in a cluttered armory, full of swords and shields, where Otello is able to eavesdrop unobserved on the conversation between Iago and Cassio amid open grillework and those implements of war that are at the heart of Otello's world. Later, when Otello has been artfully convinced by Iago that Cassio is referring to Desdemona, the armory—in one of Zeffirelli's greatest *coups de théâtre*—vanishes within seconds to reveal a vast, enclosed ceremonial hall filled with opulently dressed courtiers, bathed in warm lighting from multi-colored Moorish lamps suspended from the ceiling. When the Venetian envoys arrive in the midst of this awesome formality, the suspicious Otello cannot maintain even the barest civility required by European refinement—and before the assembled gathering he denounces his wife as unfaithful. Having been ordered by Otello to leave, the crowd disperses in horror, and from outside the Moor is hailed as the "Lion of Venice" while he is seen—the victim of a seizure—cringing on the ground. Observing him, the triumphant Iago sarcastically blurts out "Ecco il Leone!" before putting his hands on the Moor's throat intending to strangle him—only to exper-

ience a sudden pang of fear and to flee, rat-like, from the hall. This dramatic climax to Act III was seized on by many critics as being both unmotivated and dramatically ludicrous, for Verdi and Boito meant this to be Iago's moment of unadulterated triumph.

Milnes reflects, "Zeffirelli had created this love-hate relationship between the two men, which is right. Iago has a semi-struggle. He starts to strangle him and then recoils. It's that satanic, exorcist force within him, that power that makes him do it. But then Iago sees Otello down and weak, and does not want him dead. Iago does not want to be Otello—just number one to Otello. So then after putting my hands on his neck, I scuttled away like a frightened rat. I didn't take issue with that then, because I was young in the role. I did all Franco said faithfully. But it was too layered, with too many thought patterns going on—and too hard for the audience to understand. Later, I brought in the idea of defying God, making it overt, like Mefistofele defying God in Boito's opera."

While Zeffirelli maintains a stage vision of utter realism throughout the first three acts, his final scene for Act IV concentrates on stark symbolism, for Desdemona's dark bedchamber is made to resemble nothing more than a gloomy, bleak crypt or catafalque, her bed a stone slab covered with blankets and pillows. Though this seems a startling departure, Zeffirelli's idea foreshadows Desdemona's ultimate fate. It also demonstrates her removal from the rest of the castle and, at the same time, expresses her vulnerability, her lack of protection and community. In her song and prayer, she senses that her own death is close at hand, and once she has settled into bed, Otello steals into this strange forbidding room in order to take her life. With Desdemona dead on her bier, and Iago having fled, Otello then takes his dagger and, having plunged it into his side, grasps his way along the floor until he reaches Desdemona for a final kiss before he dies alongside her. The visual image thus created is one that resembles traditional *Romeo and Juliet* productions, in which the young lovers die together in the Capulet tombs.

Zeffirelli reveals to his audience a man at the end of his emotional tether, a man whose uncontrollable, volcanic rages need little prompting. While playing up Otello's brutish nature, he also conjures up the madness of a Gothic horror story, which may or may not be what Boito and Verdi had in mind in creating this tragic opera out of Shakespeare's play. The radiance of the Act I night gives way to scheming, to the inability to fathom the truth, and ultimately to murder; and the progressively closed-in, oppressive atmosphere that Zeffirelli builds up captures graphically the increasing agony of Otello's tortured soul.

Act II. The scheming Iago (Sherrill Milnes) ponders the meaning of life.

Right
Act II. Otello (Jon Vickers), governor of Crete, surrounded by maps and books.

Overleaf ▷
Act III. In the armory (*left*), Otello (Placido Domingo) delivers his impassioned monologue—"Dio! mi potevi." Following the arrival of the Venetian ambassador, Desdemona (Margaret Price) is publicly humiliated by the irate Otello and left to bemoan her fate (*right*).

Above and right

Act IV. In her crypt-like bedchamber, Desdemona (Gilda Cruz-Romo) is attended by Emilia (Shirley Love); and Otello (Placido Domingo)—overcome with remorse after smothering his wife—with his dying breath kisses her once more in farewell.

Parade: An Evening of

Production: **John Dexter**
Sets and Costumes: **David Hockney**
Lighting: **Gil Wechsler**

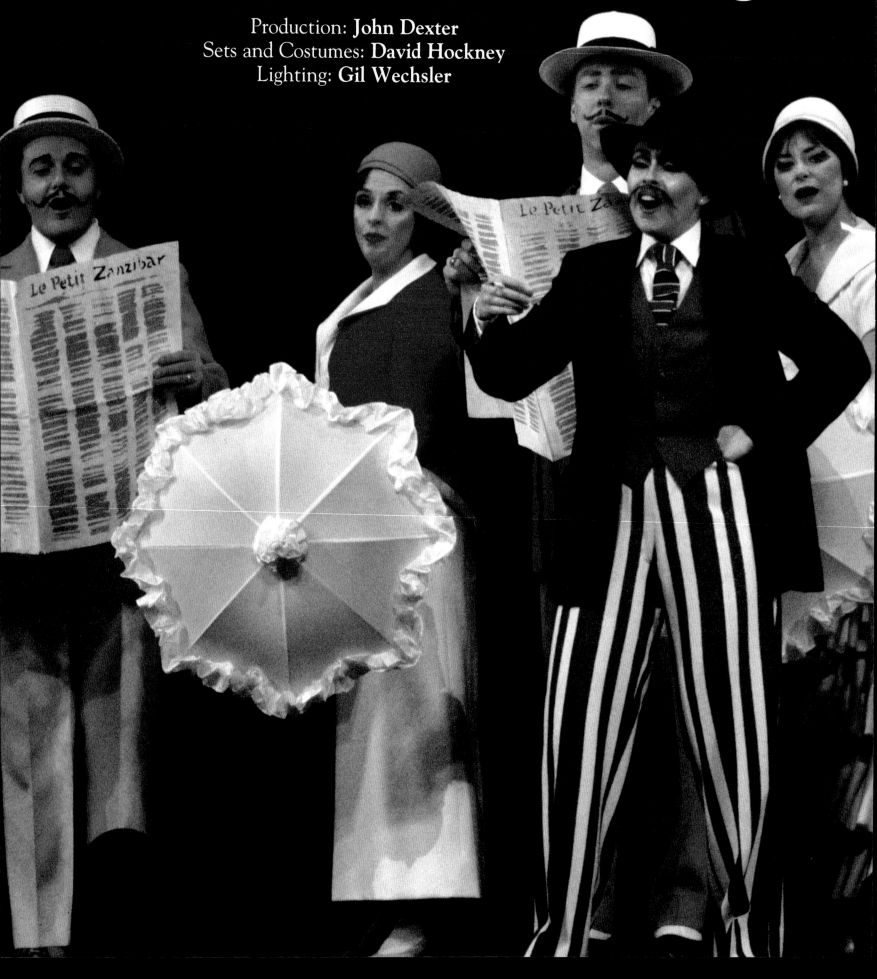

French Music Theatre

Parade
SATIE

Les Mamelles de Tirésias
POULENC

L'Enfant et les Sortilèges
RAVEL

Parade: An Evening of French Music Theatre

Parade
Les Mamelles de Tirésias
L'Enfant et les sortilèges

MANY people expressed strong doubts as to the suitability and wisdom of producing *Parade: An Evening of French Music Theatre*—would the cavernous Met be too large for such intimate, elusive works? would the public respond to a triple bill of twentieth-century music-theater novelties? would the Met meet the challenge of such a radical departure from the customary presentation of grand opera? As it turned out, this inventive collaboration between two Englishmen, the director John Dexter and the artist David Hockney proved at its premiere in February 1981 that any such fears were ill-founded. The sheer novelty of the enterprise provided the initial attraction, while its sophisticated-naïf execution assured a rousing success. A well-judged gamble paid off, and handsomely. *Parade* helped to wrench the Met into the twentieth century, a period it has only recently begun to explore in its performances. *Parade* fitted into the overall scheme laid down by

James Levine in the late 1970s when he began to oversee the artistic profile of the Met—that of exploring important works of the twentieth century while maintaining the standard repertory and looking into obscure corners of other centuries for worthwhile projects to be revived.

Dexter, who had been appointed director of productions in 1974, was by 1981 stepping down from that position. In the years between, he had put his hand to a number of works, showing strength particularly in twentieth-century repertory—Poulenc's *Dialogues des Carmélites,* Britten's *Billy Budd,* and Berg's *Lulu,* for instance—as opposed to his less felicitous approach to the standard works. In 1967, Dexter had come to the Met with an often exciting staging of Verdi's *I Vespri Siciliani* that had originated in Hamburg. This took place on the heels of a career in legitimate theater, in the course of which he worked frequently at England's National Theatre and was particularly successful as director of several new plays by Peter Shaffer. Dexter made his debut in opera with Berlioz's *Benvenuto Cellini* at Covent Garden, in 1966.

He regarded *Parade* as a kind of gala farewell party for himself, and it in turn proved to be his most affecting work at the Met. To carry out his scheme he engaged the fashionable Hockney, whose opera experience included highly pictorial sets for *The Rake's Progress* (1975) and *Die Zauberflöte* (1978) at the Glyndebourne Festival, but whose theater experience went back to 1966 and a London production of Jarry's *Ubu Roi,* when he became fascinated with creating stage sets of pictorial realism. Together with Dexter, he conjured up a very personal world with a great number of aesthetic links, threads, and connections, as well as nostalgia, in its pastiche of the modernist past. (Later, in 1983, the pair again collaborated at the Met for a Stravinsky centennial bill of *Le Sacre du printemps, Le Rossignol,* and *Oedipus Rex.*)

The three French works themselves—products of three daring composers, each of whom faced more than a little opposition to his work when it first appeared—served as a focus, for each piece looked to 1917 as a key year, the 1914–18 war as the underlying epoch. It was in 1917 that Diaghilev's Ballets Russes staged the avant-garde ballet *Parade,* with music by Erik Satie, scenario by Jean Cocteau, designs by Pablo Picasso, and choreography by Léonide Massine. It proved to be a revolutionary event in the annals of theater, and prompted the poet Guillaume Apollinaire to coin the word "surrealism." That same year, Apollinaire's play *Les Mamelles de Tirésias* had its premiere in Paris (although it had been written some years earlier)—and Francis Poulenc, who saw the play at the age of eighteen, was to set it to

Above
Hockney's finished design for
the town of Zanzibar.

music shortly after World War II. It was also in 1917, when Maurice Ravel was serving in the trenches at Verdun, that he received from Colette the libretto of the fantasy *L'Enfant et les sortilèges*. He would complete his score for it in 1925. So 1917 tied together the three elements in this Dexter-Hockney project, as did certain feelings about children, art, and fantasy amid the grim realities of war—the notion that children can redeem the world, but that they in turn must be redeemed and captivated by art. (Interestingly enough, Cocteau professed to believe that the daring of *Parade* was the greatest battle of the Great War.)

Dexter felt that the angelic, tricolor Harlequin that is introduced in *Parade* and returns at the end of *L'Enfant*—in fact, this figure was not associated with Picasso's cubist painting of this era, but was a sentimental saltimbanque of his earlier Rose Period—represents the duty of art to survive in times of crisis. "The arts," Picasso said, "are the only means by which children can grow up sane." While the symbolic child figure appears during the opening ballet, procreation amid the ravages of war is actually the subject of Poulenc's opera, and the education of an unruly child who becomes

aware of the hurt he was wrought on everything in his world is the essence of the Ravel piece. Finally, it was the decision to engage the venerable Manuel Rosenthal to conduct the three works which helped knit the whole skein together, since Rosenthal had spent his life conducting these composers' music and had studied under Ravel. Musically speaking, Satie provides the link between Ravel and Poulence, since he greatly influenced both men.

Even though some of the ideas amalgamated onstage came across as rather labored and forced, threatening to rob the three distinct works of their individuality, the total theatrical and visual effectiveness proved undeniable, appealing to the child as well as to the world citizen in every member of the audience. Most questionable was the decision to suggest an atmosphere of war in *Parade* and *Les Mamelles* via barbed wire and searchlights—even though it was fascinating historically to recall that *Parade* had indeed had its premiere at a time when German troops were less than a hundred miles from the French capital. The production was constantly making one aware that life totters between comedy and tragedy, reality and absurdity, prosperity and devastation, creation and extinction.

Overleaf ▷
Les Mamelles de Tirésias, Act I:
The Husband (David
Holloway) shows off some of
his 40,049 new progeny in
their baby carriages, and
(*inset*) Thérèse (Catherine
Malfitano) seeks freedom by
releasing her balloon breasts.

Parade. Harlequin (Gary Chryst) introduces the Child.

players enter, setting up in the midst of this war zone their little theater, the curtain of which hides portions of the sets and props for the two operas to follow. In addition to these commedia dell'arte figures, the stage becomes populated by extras dressed in pastiches of Picasso's original cubist-collage designs for the Cocteau-Massine ballet: the Chinese Conjurer, the Little American Girl, the Pantomime Horse, all in a Dadaesque sideshow of odd juxtapositions. Gray Veredon's choreography (how daunting to create afresh in the shadow of Massine's sardonic original!) amounts to little, but serves to set the stage for what is to follow, and to convey certain directorial thoughts, together with Hockney's homage to various artists of that earlier era. When Satie's typewriter is heard in the orchestra, the Harlequin pulls back a curtain to reveal a fuzzy red-haired typist busy at work— Colette herself, with her faithful cat on her desk. A pink-gloved military Death figure wearing a tin helmet and gas mask stalks through, as do the sailor-suited child from the Ravel work and various circus acrobats. The chorus, in the green garb, traditional conical headgear, and hooked-nose masks of Neapolitan Pulcinellas (inspired by Tiepolo) maneuver huge building blocks which at the end of the ballet spell out the name FRANCIS POULENC. The curtains of the little proscenium then part to introduce Poulenc's Theater Manager, dressed as Picasso's cubist pipe-smoking manager out of *Parade*.

For Poulenc's absurdist opera *Les Mamelles de Tirésias*, the small set is replaced by a larger proscenium with a crisp Dufy-inspired, mural-like setting of Zanzibar, an imaginary town with Mediterranean quay, café, and tobacconist shop, the intensely blue sky and sea background dotted with white clouds and two spiky palm trees. Hockney's deft costumes, mainly in bold stripes, are faithful to the composer's intention that they should be fantasies of Paul Poiret dresses, circa 1912. The witty farce is played out as the "feminist" Thérèse lets her two balloon breasts fly to the heavens, grows a beard and becomes a man, while the Husband proceeds to don a dress and give birth to over 40,000 children, as seen in captivating baby prams from which cardboard infants pop up, offering Apollinaire's message about making babies, not war. At the finale, dancers and singers fill the empty battlefield as they waltz nostalgically amid hundreds of red and blue balloons— a world of mammary symbolism. From a visual point of view, one feels the presence not only of Dufy and Picasso, but of Matisse, Derain, and even Marie Laurencin, with whom Apollinaire had been in love. Hockney's brilliant use of primary colors seemed to reflect his adopted California as much as the mythical Zanzibar.

As the audience enters the theater, the curtain is up on a bleak nightmare landscape of tangled barbed wire, searchlights and a bedraggled, bullet-riddled tricolor making a gallant show in the breeze. The names of the three composers are projected on the three sides of the grand proscenium arch, looking as if they had just been sprayed on as graffiti, but in fact accomplished with lighting. As the start of Satie's music, carnival

Right
Parade. The Fat Ballerina
(Gary Cordial) with the
balloon breasts of Tirésias.

Overleaf ▷
The magic garden of *L'Enfant
et les sortilèges*, with the
repentant Child (Hilda Harris)
surrounded by the animals; in
the inset the Child is seen
with his outsize story book.

Parade   171

Perhaps the greatest challenge was presented by Ravel's "lyric fantasy," *L'Enfant et les sortilèges*. So often it has proved simply impossible to stage, with its singing-and-dancing animals, furniture, books, wallpaper, and toys, which eventually teach the naughty child about compassion and love. Gone now is any sense of trench warfare, to be replaced by Hockney's own enchanted kingdom, his Fauve-inspired designs (like tempera paintings from a child's own hand) perfectly reflecting the mood of Ravel's elegantly glowing score and childlike innocence. Dexter's major decision was to place his flock of singers at either side of the proscenium, all dressed as green Pierrots, and to have dancers mime the action onstage; the result, however, sometimes proved distracting in its separation of the aural and the visual. The dancers begin with outsized play blocks, spelling out MAURICE

RAVEL, which then become the table, chairs, and fireplace of the nursery. The boy's claustrophobic, menacing room, with its exaggerated perspectives, has a darkening oppressiveness about it, the blue and purple beams threatening him. While the Mother's voice is heard, only her towering, frightening shadow can be seen. One by one the brief adventures unfold: the shepherds and shepherdesses of the boy's torn wallpaper, the princess of a fairy tale, fire, the grandfather's clock, the teacup and teapot, arithmetic and so on, all of them coming to haunt the child for his uncaring, even cruel, misdeeds.

Then, when the action switches to the garden outside, Hockney captures the evocative shimmering mystery of a summer night filled with owls, beetles, moths, and frogs, a scene of terror and delight dominated by a massive, glowing red tree

Below
The Black Cat, first seen in the ballet *Parade* (*left*), reappears in *L'Enfant et les sortilèges*, in which the Child (Hilda Harris) is scared by the Grandfather's Clock (*right*).

with leaves. Primitive-looking bats become silhouetted against an eerie purple night sky, while the green clowns assume the role of grasshoppers. Dexter takes a basically felicitous, tender approach of bemused artifice, with genial frogs and animals. Hockney, who listened to the music to seek inspiration as to shape and color, noted, "The musical description of the tree in the garden has actual weight, as a tree has. I drew the forms of the tree to the music." Working on this triple bill altered and reinforced Hockney's way of looking at his own art, particularly in relation to the Met's lighting system. Influenced primarily by Matisse in his treatment of the Ravel, he conceived the piece

as a luminous play of color, and convinced Dexter and the Met's lighting designer, Gil Wechsler, to use colored lights on painted sets of the same color, discovering that "When you put a blue light on blue paint, it comes *alive*, as something *physical*."

At the end, having bandaged the injured squirrel, the child has learned compassion, love, and understanding. He calls out for his "Maman," and the Harlequin returns to lead him into a world that, it may be hoped, will be filled with the kind of escapist fantasy, enchantment, charm, brilliance wit, stimulation, and simple fun that has been provided for the Met audience in this audacious venture.

L'Enfant et les sortilèges. The Chinese Cup and the Wedgwood Teapot indulge in nonsense dialogue.

Peter Grimes

BRITTEN

Production: **Tyrone Guthrie**
Sets and Costumes: **Tanya Moiseiwitsch**

Peter Grimes

WHEN Rudolf Bing brought Benjamin Britten's powerful and disturbing *Peter Grimes* to the new Metropolitan Opera House in January 1967, it was far more than a deserved tribute to one of this century's most brilliant composers and a work—first staged in London at Sadler's Wells in 1945—that has come to be regarded as the quintessential British opera of our time, one that gave birth to a new era of English opera. Bing was righting a wrong that went back to the regime of his predecessor, the singer turned impresario, Edward Johnson, who had first staged this opera in February 1948—but to unappreciative critics and a generally uncaring public. Now, with Sir Tyrone Guthrie's and Tanya Moiseiwitsch's stunning evocation of a fishing village in East Anglia, the tempestuous sea itself, and the harsh life of the local fishermen, the seal of success was finally put on this modern masterpiece, and it was this Met production that at long last made it possible for critics and public alike to respond to the opera's impact. *Peter Grimes* has since played all the major American opera houses—and with deserved acclaim. At the time of the 1948 Met premiere—*Peter Grimes* had been commissioned by the Koussevitzky Music Foundation and had its U.S. premiere at the Berkshire Music Center (Tanglewood) in Lenox, Massachusetts, on August 6, 1946—one critic noted that, when faced with the challenge of a modern work requiring some amount of adroitness, originality, and imagination in its presentation, the Met failed the test badly. He went on to say that it had been staged as if it were a cross between *La Gioconda* and *Die Meistersinger*; it was cast indifferently and in some cases unsuitably; and it was provided with a clutter of old-fashioned picture-book settings made up of

pasteboard houses and flickering projections of Wagnerian cloud-effects on wrinkled backdrops. Here was an opera that cried out for simplicity and directness, for stylization or at least a unity of style, in its acting and production.

Some eighteen years later, the situation was considerably altered. Bing provided Britten with all the finest ingredients imaginable to make a strikingly dramatic case for a strikingly dramatic work. Making his debut in the Met pit was the young British conductor Colin Davis, who revealed his absolute mastery of this idiom, making the score surge and soar and ebb in its continuous flow, like the sea itself, while intensifying this stark drama of human feelings, disappointments, and alienation. In the title role was one of the giants of contemporary music theater, Jon Vickers, who in the intervening years has put such a forceful stamp on the lonely, embittered, frustrated Peter Grimes that he has virtually made the role his own. With his burly, temperamental presence, Vickers—in the role of the distraught visionary—has a unique power to strike terror into the observer.

Then, to produce Britten's opera, Bing harked back to the Covent Garden premiere in 1947, when it was directed by that distinguished man of the theater, Tyrone Guthrie, and designed by Tanya Moiseiwitsch. This pair had worked together in the theater and in opera for nearly a quarter of a century by the time Guthrie died in Dublin on May 15, 1971. Years later, Miss Moiseiwitsch declared that they had attempted a highly realistic production "in a stylized sort of way, especially with the chorus on the beach at the beginning and end. It was not naturalistic," she stressed, "but let's say a heightened realism." Of their work together on the Covent Garden production, she recalled, "I had heard that Benjamin Britten felt that the settings were, to his mind, too unrealistic and gave too vague a suggestion of the village and seascape in Aldeburgh, the town he knew so well." So, for the New York production, she explained, "we made sure that Britten saw the models for the scenery before they were delivered to the Met, and he approved them all, including my detailed drawings of the characteristic lobster pot, which I had sketched on my visit to Aldeburgh."

At the time—it was the Met's first season in its new building—she and Guthrie took advantage of the vast stage and wing space, as well as the sophisticated machinery available to achieve rapid changes of scene. She recalled: "The Met's resident designer, David Reppa, was most inventive when it came to interpreting the set models. Among other things, we needed fishing nets by the mile, which were draped and festooned about the stage, and David had them woven in twine thick enough to be visible to the audience."

Above

Director Tyrone Guthrie at the Met in 1967.

◁ *Overleaf*

In the Moot Hall, at the inquest into the death of his apprentice, Grimes (Jon Vickers) gives evidence before the Borough's coroner, Swallow (Raymond Michalski). Mrs. Sedley (Jean Madeira) is on a balcony above the witness box, while Captain Balstrode (Geraint Evans) observes the proceedings at far right.

Above

Act II. The apothecary Keene (Gene Boucher), with Auntie (Lili Chookasian) and the fisherman Boles (Paul Franke).

Left

Act II, Scene 1. Among the townspeople leaving the church after Sunday-morning service are the widow Mrs. Sedley (Jean Kraft) and the lawyer Swallow (Jerome Hines).

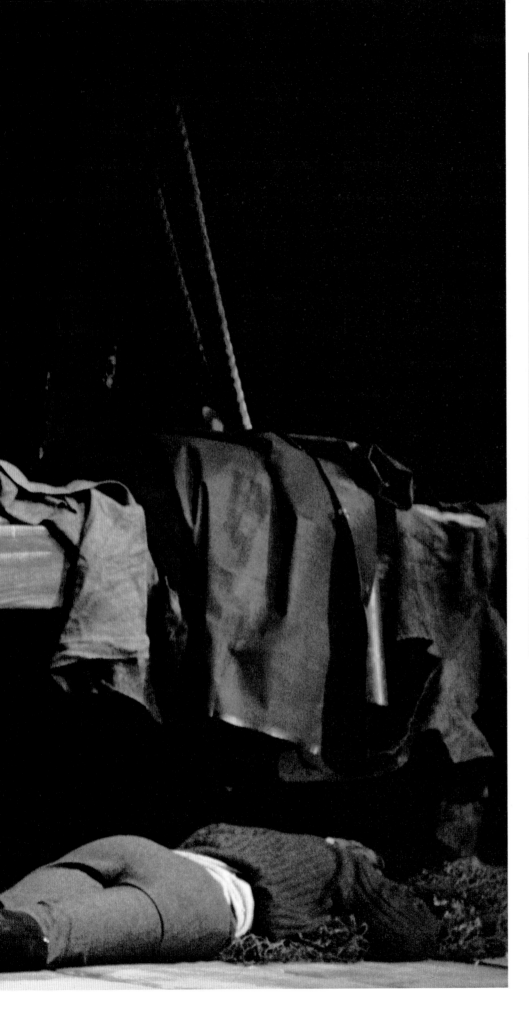

Above
Costume design for Grimes by Tanya Moiseiwitsch.

Left
Act II, Scene 2. In his hut, Grimes (Jon Vickers) is haunted by memories of the death of his first apprentice, as his new boy lies asleep on the floor.

Guthrie had worked at the Met twice previously: on his controversial but revolutionary *Carmen* in 1952, with decor by Rolf Gérard; and, in 1957, on *La Traviata*, with Renata Tebaldi, and decor by Oliver Smith. Throughout the vast range of his work for the stage, whether lyric or legitimate, Guthrie's primary objective had been to create the illusion of humanity. His sympathy with actors, and his desire for them to portray the most natural, human characters onstage, began early. Born in Tunbridge Wells on July 2, 1900, he was engaged by the director of the Oxford University Dramatic Society for the leading role in a play by George Bernard Shaw, after which he gave up acting to turn to every other aspect of the theater, culminating in his artistic direction of the Old Vic in London, starting in 1933, and the founding of the Guthrie Theater in Minneapolis in 1963.

Guthrie consistently deplored the fact that opera was getting grander and grander, more and more expensive, further and further out of touch with contemporary life and art. In 1967, he recalled: "Years ago, when I was administrator of the Sadler's Wells Opera in London, I tried gradually to effect a few changes in the direction of making opera simpler and less old-fashioned, of catering less to the myth of the fashionable wealthy patron, who even then had long since defected to the ballet. My most vehement opponents were those who would, I thought, have the most to gain by the changes I sought to effect—the singers and musicians. When in 1945 the management decided to put on the first production of Benjamin Britten's *Peter Grimes*, the idea was regarded by the company as completely laughable, even scandalous. Most of the singers found it unintelligible and outrageous that the company's future should be staked upon a work by a young man barely thirty years of age and still unknown to fame. The more musically enlightened thought it a marvelous score but were positive it would never 'take.' How, they urged (not unreasonably), will it ever be accepted by the public which still wants *Madama Butterfly* and Gounod's *Faust*? The answer is, first, that the British public did, and does, accept it; second, that an opera house whose most modern works are those of Puccini, over two generations old, is not doing its job."

Much the same thing happened in New York, around 1967. The public suddenly took *Peter Grimes* to its heart, and the Met was certainly doing its job by bringing back this work and giving it a production worthy of its stature. In New York *Grimes* finally achieved the respect and even love it should have had in the years that separated its two local productions. As opera it is both powerful and unique, for the work is a splendid example of psychological music theater: a study in frustration

Left

Act I, Scene 3. At the Boar Inn, during a storm, Grimes (Jon Vickers) poetically raves "Now the Great Bear and Pleiades," perplexing the others present, who include Balstrode (Geraint Evans) and Auntie (Lili Chookasian). On the left are one of Auntie's "Nieces" (Mary Ellen Pracht) and, with his back turned, Boles (Paul Franke).

Overleaf ▷

Act III. The quayside in Scene 2, as the townspeople go about their daily business. The inset shows Grimes's only friends in the Borough, Balstrode (Geraint Evans) and the schoolmistress Ellen Orford (Lucine Amara).

Act II, Scene 1. Ellen Orford (Elisabeth Söderström) asks John, Grimes's new apprentice (Kirk Peterson), about a bruise on his neck.

and madness growing out of the environmental forces of the sea, from which Grimes wrests a living, and of the society of the Borough, in which he is forced to exist as an isolated outsider. As a result of his own life outside the Establishment—as a homosexual, as a pacifist and conscientious objector during World War II, during which he exiled himself for a time in the U.S.—Britten found a tremendously responsive chord in the poetry of George Crabbe, a nineteenth-century native of the composer's adopted town, Aldeburgh. It was the novelist Montagu Slater who adapted Crabbe's "The Borough" (1810), which became the basis of *Peter Grimes*. And as much as the outcast Grimes is the protagonist of the work, so—as in Mussorgsky's *Boris Godunov*—is the chorus, the composite of townsfolk whose scandal-mongering, hostility, and bigotry lead to Grimes's final catastrophe once he has been found responsible for the death of his two apprentices.

Peter Grimes is a work of both stark reality and soaring poetry, and these two seemingly conflicting aspects are expertly reconciled in the Guthrie–Moiseiwitsch production. The opera begins, *in medias res*, with the coroner's inquest into the "accidental" disappearance of Grimes's young apprentice. Instantly, as the curtain rises for the Prologue, the audience is faced with a setting of harsh, dour reality: the beamed courtroom in the Moot Hall, where the townsfolk are crowded to hear Grimes's halting, tense story of how the boy died at sea. The sturdiness of the hall and its utilitarian air epitomize the need for every structure in the Borough to be able to withstand the ravages of storms and relentlessly harsh weather. Such is the view outside the hall when, in Act I, Scene 1, the drops of fishermen's nets reveal the gray, weathered timbers of the pier looming above the slip outside "The Boar" tavern, and narrow, steep, stone streets. Against a grim sky, women are mending nets and sails while the fishermen prepare their boats for the day, all going about their duties grimly, mechanically, as if their way of life were in some way preordained, and not open to question. One can almost feel the salty spray of the North Sea.

The setting inside "The Boar" for the storm in Scene 2 reiterates that feeling of raw strength of a structure that has withstood every cruelty nature can inflict on man. With ceiling lights swinging as the wind rages and rain pouring in every time the pub door opens, Guthrie's direction makes the audience feel the huddling together for comfort and support of this close-knit society, as it awaits Grimes and the arrival of his new apprentice, delivered to the fisherman by Ellen Orford, the gentle schoolteacher he wants to marry. Once in this milieu and out of the crushing storm, Grimes sings poetically and mysteriously "Now the Great Bear and Pleiades," a passage which serves to show how different he is from those around him.

In Act II, the gaunt atmosphere of the beach and pier is again in evidence for the gentle scene between Ellen and the new boy, who is suddenly and cruelly dragged off by Grimes to work—even on Sunday, when the townspeople gather in church. Then, after Grimes has violently argued with Ellen and hauled the bruised boy back to his hut, the men band together in search of him, singing a drum-punctuated chant. In Scene 2, Grimes's small, poor hut is revealed, set precariously on a rocky precipice with steep, weathered wooded steps on both sides and support posts rotting away through exposure to the severe elements. Here, with the men approaching and Grimes eager to set sail, the boy accidentally slips and falls to his death in a dramatic climax, made even more chilling by the entry of the men into the now empty hut.

For the final act, the setting is again that of the waterfront, outside Auntie's tavern, as the villagers, still puzzled, discuss the disappearance of Grimes and the boy. And here, in this foggy ambience, when Peter returns, Captain Balstrode convinces the mad fisherman to submit to his fate and take his boat out to sea and sink it before he is caught by the search party. Then, as the new day dawns, the people of the Borough almost mechanically resume their daily activities, as if nothing—not even a boat sinking out at sea—could disturb the cycle of battling against the elements, surviving, and eking out a living. The disturbing, aggressive, psychopathic misfit, yearning for peace, has vanished, but the Borough remains as unchanging as the sea that both nourishes and batters it.

For the magically descriptive sea interludes, which provide a gripping continuity, Moiseiwitsch designed a multiple-level drop curtain of fishermen's nets, which keep the audience's attention focused on that ever-present image of the sea and man's dependence on it, as the orchestra describes the various moods of the sea. Her costumes seem to be inspired by the subdued colors of the wood and stones of the village, as well as by their function, a bright contrast being provided by the splash of royal blue of Ellen's dress.

Guthrie succeeded handsomely in creating a microcosm of English seaside life, with its violently changing moods and actions. In his unrelenting staging, he vividly balances the hard, unfeeling character of most of the villagers with the compassionate figures of Ellen and Balstrode, Grimes's wise and faithful friend. Every member of the cast evinces a distinct character and personality, and likewise the individual characters of the old-maidish widow, Mrs. Sedley, the frowsy Auntie with her two tarty "nieces," the Methodist preacher Bob Boles, and the joking Ned Keene are all successfully brought to life. Together they form a convincing community, drawing the viewer into this drama of isolation and barebones existence with startling realism—yet maintaining the poetry which raises the whole of Britten's opera into an exalted theatrical experience.

Act III, Scene 2. As Balstrode (Geraint Evans) watches, Ellen (Lucine Amara) cradles the prostrate Grimes (Jon Vickers), before he goes out to sea to sink his boat.

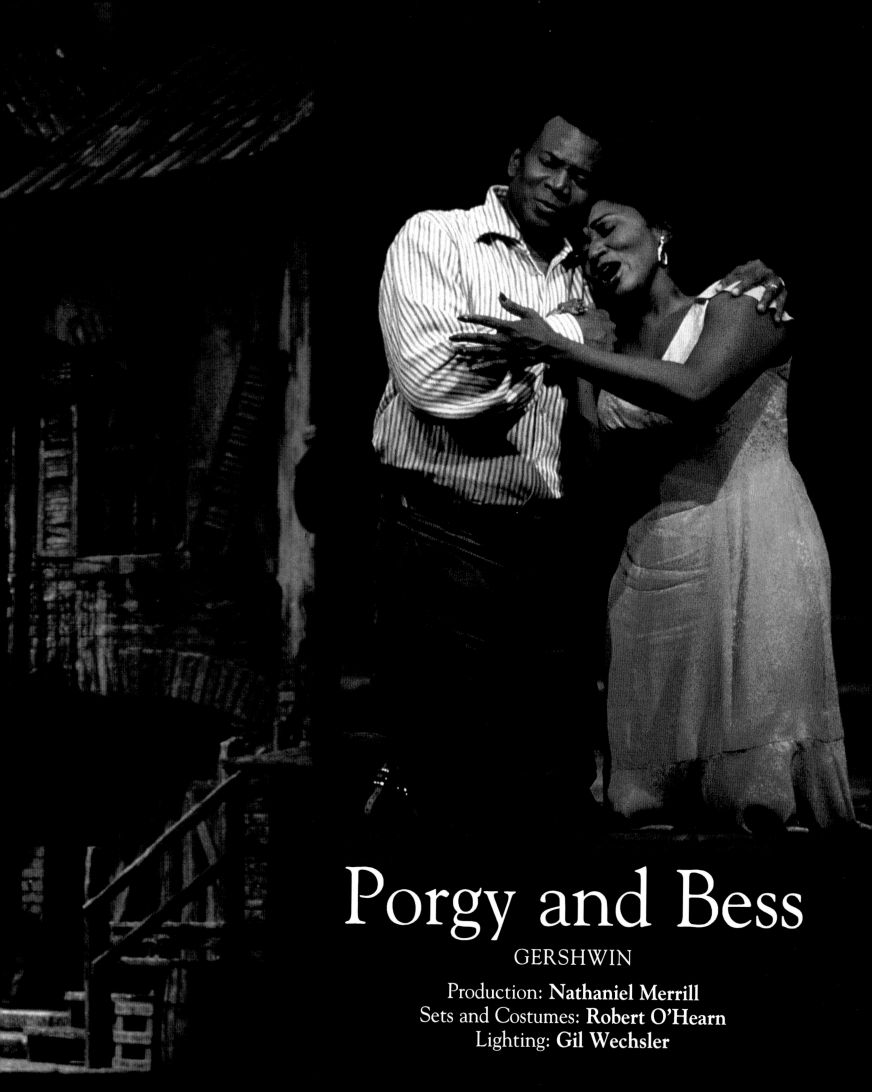

Porgy and Bess

GERSHWIN

Production: **Nathaniel Merrill**
Sets and Costumes: **Robert O'Hearn**
Lighting: **Gil Wechsler**

Porgy and Bess

Above
Designer Robert O'Hearn and director Nathaniel Merrill between rehearsals.

◁ *Overleaf*
In Act III, Scene 2, the Coroner (Hansford Rowe) questions Lily (Priscilla Baskerville), Serena (Florence Quivar), and Maria (Barbara Conrad) about the murder of Crown. During the second act (*right*), Porgy (Simon Estes) and Bess (Grace Bumbry) pledge their love—"Bess, You Is My Woman Now."

GEORGE GERSHWIN's songs "Summertime," "My Man's Gone Now," "Bess, You Is My Woman Now," "I Loves You Porgy," "I Got Plenty o' Nuttin'," "It Ain't Necessarily So"—with lyrics by his brother Ira and DuBose Heyward—have long been a part of the American consciousness, ever since *Porgy and Bess* had its premiere on Broadway under the auspices of the Theatre Guild at the Alvin Theater on October 10, 1935, following previews in Boston. For years, these remarkable melodies, so eloquent in their harmony and rhythmic pulse, and these lyrics were perceived as part of an opera-style work that had proved to be a commercial failure; the first *Porgy and Bess* ran for only 124 performances, and in 1937, when George Gershwin succumbed to a brain tumor, he died believing that his most ambitious composition was a failure. The work involved a number of anomalous forces: as a black piece created by whites, as an opera staged on Broadway, as a score utilizing "classical" and pop techniques, even as the joint creation of a Southern aristocrat and a New York Jew.

A successful revival seven years later—with severe cuts and the recitative turned into spoken dialogue—lasted for some 286 performances, but only recently has *Porgy and Bess* become accepted for what it really is, a true American folk opera, both serious and accessible. At one point, because of his friendship with Otto Kahn, board chairman of the Metropolitan Opera, the composer thought that, when completed, *Porgy and Bess* might be headed for that temple of high art on West 39th Street; but Kahn's death in 1934 put an end to any such fantasies. It would take fifty years for *Porgy and Bess* finally to reach the place where it rightfully belongs, the Metropolitan Opera, and its arrival on February 6, 1985, was due to music director James Levine's belief in the work: "It's a masterpiece, a true work of art, a great work of American art. It was clearly conceived by its creators as an opera, as opposed to a Broadway show. We're dealing with a work that the creator never saw in the form he conceived for it." Levine alludes to the fact that Gershwin conceived and wrote *Porgy and Bess* as an opera with traditional recitative instead of dialogue to link the arias, duets, and ensembles. Most revivals not only severely trimmed the work, but also replaced these recitatives with Broadway-style dialogue. Only in the 1976 Houston Grand Opera production, which toured the U.S. and Europe extensively, did the original form of *Porgy and Bess* resurface, albeit slightly cut—but performed by opera singers and a full orchestra. Levine brought the complete work to the Met just as Gershwin had envisioned it, and he shakes his head over that nagging question, "Is it an opera?" He views such doubts as utter nonsense: "It is a superb opera, and it has everything great opera has—great music, great drama, and a psychological social milieu that is as involving as the milieu of *Don Giovanni* or *Boris Godunov*."

Porgy and Bess opened at the Met with a whole skein of sociological meanings and justifications. Long thought to represent a stereotype of poor rural blacks, the opera had transcended that small-minded reaction. The story, as introduced by DuBose Heyward in a 1925 novel, *Porgy*, then adapted for the stage in 1927, tells of a crippled beggar, a drug-addicted whore, a sexy murderer (Crown), and a snake-like tempter (Sporting Life). These characters have entered into American folklore, just as Gershwin's often folklorish music has become part of the American musical mainstream. *Porgy and Bess* is a work that has rarely been produced in an opera house, but rather in the theater—despite touring editions that landed at La Scala or even the Bolshoi Theater in Moscow, as did the famous 1952 production that toured four continents in six years. For the Met, the arrival of *Porgy and Bess* seemed to symbolize a whole new age of acceptance of the American black singer, a trend dramatically begun in 1955 when Rudolf Bing sponsored Marian Anderson as the first black to sing at the house. Since that time, the position and acceptance of the black singer have been evolving slowly and significantly, and during the Levine regime a veritable blossoming of black singers on the Met's roster has taken place before our eyes. This is a far cry from the days when revivals of *Porgy and Bess* provided virtually the only source of livelihood and exposure available to budding black artists.

Right
During the Overture, the fisherman Jake (Bruce Hubbard) listens as his wife Clara (Myra Merritt) sings the lullaby "Summertime."

Left
Act I, Scene 1. The crap game heats up: Bess (Grace Bumbry), Robbins (Donald Osborne), Jake (Bruce Hubbard), Jim (Michael Smartt, standing), Mingo (John A. Freeman-McDaniels), Crown (Gregg Baker), Sporting Life (Charles Williams), and Porgy (Simon Estes).

Overleaf ▷
Act I, Scene 2. (*Inset*) Serena (Florence Quivar) mourns her dead husband Robbins—"My Man's Gone Now." After a visit from the police, Bess (Grace Bumbry) leads a hymn about the journey to the promised land—"Oh, The Train Is At The Station"; Maria (Barbara Conrad) is at Bess's right, with Lily (Priscilla Baskerville) seated at the table, and Porgy (Simon Estes) on the floor.

Porgy and Bess 191

Above and opposite

Act II, Scene 1. Porgy (Simon Estes), Archdale (Gary Drane), and the inhabitants of Catfish Row sight a buzzard—a sign of bad luck; and Porgy cheerfully proclaims "I Got Plenty o' Nuttin'."

Bringing *Porgy and Bess* to the Met proved no easy task. The Gershwin estate insists on an all-black cast for the work, both principals and chorus. Since the Met's chorus is predominantly white, an entirely new choral ensemble of seventy had to be auditioned, assembled, and trained for the sixteen performances given in the first season. While many of the roster's leading black singers would take leading roles—Simon Estes as Porgy (who, after an accident to his knee during the fight scene in the dress rehearsal, had to play the first night on crutches), Grace Bumbry as Bess, Florence Quivar as Serena, Myra Merritt as Clara, for instance—others had to be engaged for such key parts as Sporting Life and Crown (Charles Williams and Gregg Baker respectively).

Whereas previous productions had effected a delicate balance between Broadway and opera house styles—Gershwin proved to be a "crossover" creator decades before that phrase even existed—the Met took a decidedly opera-house approach to the work, giving it a massiveness of production and musical style. For its production team, it called on two veterans of the Met from the early 1960s onward, director Nathaniel Merrill and designer Robert O'Hearn, who had worked together in the house on eight previous occasions. They had also staged the Gershwin work twice in Europe, in 1966 for the Vienna Volksoper and in 1969 for the Bregenz Festival, both with black soloists but a local chorus whose members had to wear what is called in the theater "Texas dirt" makeup.

Merrill feels that fifty years after its premiere *Porgy and Bess* emerges as a pro-black piece, without the Jim Crow image it possessed in the 1950s. "It's now solid Americana, 'How the East was won,' in a way. It's part of our folklore—a folk opera, which is what Gershwin wanted to write. So it has come into its own. It's a piece about real Americans in our history who happen to be black, but they could have been Chinese or Hispanic or whatever." The Gullahs portrayed are a special minority group, a race of Africans who settled in the U.S. and have their own colorful brand of English. They transplanted their civilization to America, and their isolated tribal ways of life and religion, separated from the urban world, fascinated Gershwin. Merrill and O'Hearn decided to set the tale in the 1930s of the Depression, the time of the play and the opera, even though the Heyward novel puts it in 1911. O'Hearn supplied the highly realistic settings, from the picturesque though battered slums of Catfish Row with its gated bridge, to the shabby room of Serena, conveying a former architectural grandeur, to the tropical paradise of Kittiwah Island, just off the coast from Charleston. In these authentic sets the drama of innocence in a fierce struggle with nature and the social forces that surround the Gullahs is played full-out.

Merrill sees the director's task as a difficult one, since most of the cast are either onstage for the greater part of the evening, or are getting ready to go onstage. "There are no relaxing sections, because everyone is always doing something. It's like doing four first acts of *Carmen*. *Porgy and Bess* is a naturalistic piece that takes tremendous detail of invention for the chorus, which is onstage from beginning to end, except for the few arias or duets. With nineteen or twenty soloists, it's a big cast. And there are no comprimarios as in Verdi, with a servant or gardener. They go through the entire opera. They may not be singing, but they are there as part of the whole society, the teeming life onstage. Basically, it's a big, complex evening for the director. It takes a long rehearsal time, which we got at the Met. We had a new chorus that had never done *Porgy* before, and many of the soloists had never performed it either. It was not like doing a work where the tenor, soprano, and baritone have sung their parts here and there and then come with ideas from other productions. So it took time to get it organized. And the chorus, representative of a black society, is a strong protagonist, as it is in *Peter Grimes* or *Boris Godunov*."

Merrill feels that his staging differs from earlier ones, in that he sees the tragedy as being that of Bess, "because she cannot settle for the goodness of the crippled Porgy, who outwardly is not a good-looking, whole man. And she is unable to live with the handsome sensuality of Crown, a seductive whole man who is not good, because he murders Robbins, but who is also not a coward, because he goes after Clara in the storm. Bess can't settle for either one and goes off to New York with Sporting Life to be a prostitute. That's the tragedy. Usually Crown is played as a super-unintelligent, mean, ugly character with few redeeming characteristics, but there's an erotic love duet for the two, so you have to feel his sexual magnetism. He's appealing, even though he's a bully and a killer. But Bess likes being bullied. It's a relationship they both want. At Kittiwah, where he's hiding out from the police, he doesn't seduce and rape her. As I see it, it is *she* who rapes him at the end. She is not forced to stay. She stays because she wants to."

Act II, Scene 2. After the church picnic on Kittiwah Island, Crown (Gregg Baker), sought for the murder of Robbins, comes out of hiding (*left*) to find Bess, but first Sporting Life (Charles Williams) tells the true believers of the congregation "It Ain't Necessarily So" (*above*).

In the final scene of Act II (*right*), as the hurricane rages, all the citizens of Catfish Row pray—"Oh, De Lawd Shake De Heavens."

Act III. Sporting Life (Charles Williams) persuades Bess (Grace Bumbry), to whom he has given drugs, that the good life can be hers by going with him to New York.

is a sense of vulnerability as the folk face the elements in an aged, rickety structure.

Merrill believes that doing *Porgy and Bess* as an opera, not as a Broadway show, means believing in its musical values. "You make things happen without extraneous business. You rely on the music . . . and don't intrude on it." Indeed, this Met version of the Gershwin classic often has an operatic look to it, with static moments as opposed to the action-filled direction of previous versions. But Merrill explains, "For certain episodes there is little action because we have small playing areas full of people—like the scene in Serena's room and then the hurricane. People are packed in like sardines, and this sense of oppressiveness is right for these moments. You don't need a lot of running around."

The technically sophisticated Met stage allowed the production team to create many effects not possible on Broadway or with a touring edition. They were able to make use of stage elevators, the revolving stage, and sliding stages. Probably the most noticeable variation comes at the very beginning of the work with the three scene-setting vignettes that serve as a prologue, with Jasbo Brown's jazz, Serena singing "Summertime," and the gambling scene, before the action proper begins. Merrill sees this as a prologue because the plot has not yet begun and it's not yet real Catfish Row. Jasbo Brown offers the feeling of ennui, the repetitive music reflecting the boredom of Charleston waterfront life. "Summertime" provides a sweet, romantic tableau removed from realism, and the gambling is a fateful foretelling of what will happen in the opera itself when Crown kills Robbins in a drunken row. Merrill feels that these are unrealistic moments, and unrelated to the piece. Using the raised elevator stage, he provides a kind of Brechtian alienation sequence before the real Catfish Row music begins and one is plunged right into the action, the main characters being introduced in logical, methodical fashion by Gershwin—Jake, Robbins and Serena, Jim, Porgy, Bess, and Crown, all in a dramaturgical pattern. Also, at the beginning of the second scene in Serena's room, after Robbins has been murdered by Crown, Merrill makes use of stylization as each person who knew Robbins talks philosophically about him and about death. Each is lit up individually and set apart from the crowd before the lights go up on the full scene. Merrill sees these as "poetic visions," different from the common mass mourning, and he uses each in turn as a kind of bridge, so that the scene changes can be made easily and quickly. The important thing with *Porgy and Bess*, he stresses, is that "it is a cumulative piece, with one thing after another. It has to keep moving, nonstop."

Merrill and O'Hearn pursued the traditional realistic way of staging *Porgy and Bess*, although the director admits it could be done in quite another manner. The team felt that Catfish Row is a real place, as described by Heyward. The area was originally one of fancy city houses belonging to Charleston whites, and these houses were eventually taken over by the blacks who turned them into slum tenements. (Today they have been reclaimed and make up part of Charleston's most elegant neighborhood.) It is a concentrated area of too many people crowded into one place, and hence there has to be a sense of clutter and disarray. One unusual aspect was the special scene designed by O'Hearn for the hurricane episode, usually played back in Serena's room, where the mourning for Robbins had taken place. "We felt these people are threatened," reasons Merrill, "so they get as close to the sea and storm as possible. We set it in a fisherman's shanty on pilings next to the water." In this way the audience can feel the storm and sky around the denizens of Catfish Row. The lightning, too, can be palpably felt, rather than glimpsed through the broken slats of a room. There

A fierce sense of vindication accompanied the Met premiere of Gershwin's final work for the theater, the summation of a prodigious career on Broadway and in Hollywood that began in 1919. *Porgy and Bess* has taken its place as a classic, although critics a half-century ago were not quite sure what it was. Its catholic derivation confused and angered critics, particularly music critics who condemned it, despite Gershwin's innate comprehension of the variety of the black idiom. The adroit fusion of Heyward's play and Gershwin's endless fascination with jazz and black music is just another case of a visionary ahead of his time. It took the end of the Depression and a second world war before America began seriously considering its roots and developing nationalistic feelings in its performing arts. Jerome Kern's brilliant *Show Boat*

(1927)—with its Mississippi riverboat life out of Edna Ferber's novel—serves as a bridge to this aspect of Americana through works of Marc Blitzstein, Rodgers and Hart, Rodgers and Hammerstein, Leonard Bernstein, Virgil Thomson, Kurt Weill, Frank Loesser, Jule Styne, Stephen Sondheim, and others. Many of their creations have become part of the whole genre of musical theater that is now vigorously embraced by American opera companies.

Critic Martin Gottfried likens *Porgy and Bess* to the paintings of Edward Hopper in its mythic, surreal sense of a bygone America, and Bernstein calls Gershwin "one of the true authentic geniuses American music has produced." The arrival of *Porgy and Bess* at the Met signifies that America's own heritage has come of age.

Act III. In the finale, Porgy (Simon Estes) sets off with his goat-drawn cart in search of Bess—"Oh Lawd, I'm On My Way." Behind Porgy is old Peter (Mervin Wallace); to his left is Mingo (John A. Freeman-McDaniels), and to his right Lily (Priscilla Baskerville).

I Puritani

BELLINI

Production: **Sandro Sequi**   Sets: **Ming Cho Lee**
Costumes: **Peter J. Hall**

I Puritani

Above
Costume design by Peter J. Hall for Elvira in Act I, Scene 3, showing the bridal veil.

◁ *Overleaf*
Act I, Scene 2. Elvira (Joan Sutherland) with her uncle Giorgio (James Morris), as he reveals that it is thanks to him that her father has agreed to the match with Arturo—"Sorgea la notta folta."

VINCENZO BELLINI told Carlo Pepoli, the librettist for *I Puritani*, "Opera must make people weep, shudder, die through the singing." In terms of the Romantic sensibility of the early 1830s, when the young composer completed what was to prove his final opera, *I Puritani* has exactly this emotional power to transport an audience, despite its problematic, even ridiculous libretto. It is rare today for the bel canto operas of this era to reach the stage in the spirit in which they were originally conceived. Conductors, directors, and designers seem reluctant to trust these frail dramatic statements, and the slender, elegiac, melodic line, which was designed to provide a vehicle for exquisite singing. How triumphant, then, was the new production of *I Puritani* in 1976, the first appearance at the Met since 1918 of this masterwork. It had an ecstatic reception, similar to the one it must have had in its own day, for this production plumbed the essence of the work, never for a moment doubting its effectiveness, never underplaying out of embarrassment or overplaying out of doubt. Everything about it seemed right, making it the nearest thing to a perfect incarnation of a bel canto opera within living memory.

To begin with, the Met had assembled as principals perhaps the finest cast available anywhere at that moment, a four-star quartet able to walk confidently in the footsteps of Grisi, Rubini, Tamburini, and Lablache, who had created the work. Bellini's music, of course, exists first and foremost for its bel canto qualities, and the four leads—Joan Sutherland, Luciano Pavarotti, Sherrill Milnes, and James Morris—did every moment of the score proud, while conductor Richard Bonynge brought to it his expert knowledge of works of the Romantic era. Designer Ming Cho Lee captured the Romantic atmosphere in simple but highly evocative settings, misty in detail, pastel in inspired colorations (subtle grays, pale greens, white, beige), never heavy (even when the emphasis was on stonework for castles and fortresses), but providing an ideal arena for singing and acting. Lee is one of the few designers active today who have a true sense of the architectural. For this production he successfully scaled down the vast volume of the Met stage so that attention would not be diverted from the drama involving the four principals. Peter J. Hall designed costumes of imaginative elegance and taste that superbly fitted into the total visual picture, particularly his white-satin creations for the members of the wedding party, the rich velvet capes for the Cavaliers, the gracious gowns for Elvira, and the severely proper dress for the opposing Roundheads.

Finally, this production was fortunate in having as its director Sandro Sequi, no novice in the presentation of bel canto operas. Here, he managed to make the early-nineteenth-century stage conventions come gracefully and thrillingly alive. Each scene emerged like an old-master painting or a hand-colored lithograph of the era. He had principals and chorus move with a delicate ease, each pose and gesture entirely suited to the spirit of the music. Colors, lighting, movement, attitude, everything went into a vibrant embodiment of that elusive Romantic spirit.

Joan Sutherland has specialized in dramatic roles, including that of Elvira, through the years, and she can swoon and achieve fights of madness with the best of them. Here, Sequi had her seeking not Actors Studio realism, but a gentle feyness that is exactly right for this vague young lady in whom lucidity and madness alternate so readily. Sequi's ideas were almost all apt, including a succession of picturesque groupings. In Act I he used the *polacco* of "Son vergin vezzosa" to bring the white-clad teenagers of the wedding party together, and Elvira's madness at the close of the act found her theatrically letting the wedding bouquet crumble in her hands as her hair fell around her shoulders (in a manner reminiscent of *Giselle*, Act I). Lee's steep staircase for Act II gave Elvira's centerpiece mad scene, "Qui la voce," an appropriate area in which she could move with touching simplicity and ease, gradually coming toward the audience and drawing them closer to her in her plight. All this was bathed in soft, dappled lighting conceived by Sequi and Lee, the final ingredient of an exquisite, magical whole.

While Sequi has long directed operas of all periods, he has made a name for himself especially in the bel canto canon, directing such rarities as: Rossini's *Otello* at the Rome Opera; *L'Assedio di Corinto* at La Scala and later the Met; *Semiramide* at Florence's Maggio Musicale and in Chicago; and *Guillaume Tell* in Florence; as well as Bellini's *Norma* at Covent Garden and *I Puritani* in Bologna, Florence, Naples, and Rome; and Donizetti's *Fausta* in Rome and *La Fille du régiment* at Covent Garden and then the Met (his debut in the theater in 1972). Of the Bellini repertory he has also directed *La Sonnambula* (his first major assignment, at La Fenice, Venice, the success of which brought his highly musical approach to notice), *I Capuleti e i Montecchi*, and the early *Bianca e Fernando*. He feels a special affinity with such works, as he does with what he calls "all psychologically subtle works, including the plays of Goethe and Racine," which he has also directed. Over the years he has remained fascinated with bel canto in its historical context, deriving as it does from Mozart "as the first romantic and last classical composer and going straight into early Verdi.".

Above

Act I, Scene 2. Elvira (Joan Sutherland) hears her uncle, Giorgio (James Morris), laud her wedding day.

Left

Act I, Scene 3. Elvira (Joan Sutherland) displays the veil—"Son vergin vezzosa."

Act I. The set for the Puritan
fortress in Scene 1 (*above*), as
Riccardo (Sherrill Milnes),
whose hopes of marrying
Elvira have been thwarted,
sings "O Elvira, o mio sospir
soave."

In Act I, Scene 3 (*right*),
Arturo (Luciano Pavarotti),
newly arrived at the castle,
greets his future bride Elvira
(Joan Sutherland) with "A te,
o cara."

In Act II (*left*), Riccardo
(Sherrill Milnes) and Giorgio
(James Morris) contemplate
the sad fate of Elvira and
Riccardo.

Opposite

Act II. Elvira (Joan
Sutherland), abandoned by
Arturo, makes her
impassioned plea for him to
return—"Qui la voce."

When he entered this rarified world with Rossini's *Otello* back in 1964, he chose the celebrated surrealist painter Giorgio de Chirico to reconstruct the atmosphere of the early nineteenth century through Delacroix-inspired paintings. As he concluded, "These operas don't work dramatically with an independent life of their own, but must be understood through the eyes of their own *epoca*. They remain far from us, but we must look back on them with nostalgia, with love and affection. They need the help of this historic 'frame,' through which modern audiences can see these operas. Since they are often contrary to real drama, as such they provide pleasure for the ears first, then the eyes. The most beautiful bel canto point of view is the music, so a director has to cope with a definite lack of dramaturgy, that inner dramatic tension. And yet there is almost always some inner dramatic tension that must be brought out in a production. In *I Puritani* the climactic dramatic moment is Elvira's 'Qui la voce,' where bel canto completely fuses with something real and profound. It is the suffering of a young human soul, and hence the drama. But if a director does not know the weak spots of a work and believes in a drama that isn't there, he can do incredibly bad service to it."

The director in the twentieth century has to help a work such as *I Puritani*, Sequi insists. His

approach is simple: he makes it stylistically grand and leaves sufficient space for the singers and the music itself, seeing it somewhat like "a grand concert in costumes, with delicate lighting." Sequi feels that a director must bring to Rossini, for instance, a clarity of vision with bright, clear lighting to illuminate the detail of the highly theatrical passions of a precise mechanism. In the present case, however, "what must come out onstage is a feeling of sentiment, of delicate passions typical of Bellini. It is like Chopin's music being played in an intimate salon versus a large concert hall. So *I Puritani* at the Met was a big problem, for the theater is enormous. With Bellini you must make the public come nearer to the music and drama. The audience should feel near this fragile, almost nonexistent drama, this plot, the exquisite characters in the opera. To achieve this, I used tableaux with warm lighting, an atmosphere of sunset, an evanescent world that almost disappears from sight. There is a great quality of poetry in Bellini. It is not powerful, but intense, rich in texture." Pursuing this, Sequi talked to designer Lee about taking Turner paintings as a source of inspiration, and Lee responded admirably to the basic concept—as did longtime colleague Peter Hall, who matched Lee's color and period sense in a highly appropriate style.

Below

Act I, Scene 3. As Enrichetta
(Cynthia Munzer) watches,
Arturo (Luciano Pavarotti)
and Riccardo (Sherrill Milnes)
prepare to duel.

Act I, Scene 3. Set design by Ming Cho Lee for the Puritan fortress, where the betrothal party gathers (*above*). Her intended bridegroom Arturo having fled, Elvira (Joan Sutherland) loses her reason in the Mad Scene—"O vieni al tempio."

Sequi had first put his hand to *I Puritani* at Bologna's Teatro Comunale in 1969 (with Pavarotti, and with designs by Jürgen Henze). At that time too, Turner had provided the principal inspiration. Before his collaboration on the 1976 production, Lee had rarely taken a painterly approach to his sets, but in this case he enthusiastically accepted the concept of Turner and his evocative tone painting. While he had previously worked almost exclusively with three-dimensional models, Lee here steeped himself in real sketches and painting. As Sequi has stressed time and again, it became a question of conveying the "atmosphere" of the work. Yes, it is an opera for singers, but the living drama onstage has to unfold in the special atmosphere the music creates. Joan Sutherland wanted not only to sing but to act the role of Elvira, and she and Sequi worked together for a week before official rehearsals began, constructing a moving character distressed by passion and sweetly mad, as conceived by Bellini. "It was my idea," offers Sequi, "that in operas of this period the character is always a great singer *and* the personage—in this case, Elvira. The singers of that era brought their own costumes and jewelry, which were not historically correct but contemporary to the opera. So a director must forget his ego a little and follow the dictates of the work. That is the only way to give full life to these operas."

How to deal with the limited stage action? Sequi concedes that *I Puritani* does not possess the full inner drama of, say, *Don Giovanni*, *Fidelio* or *Otello*. "A director," he says, "has to work hard to avoid anything ridiculous onstage. The duel at the end of Act I, for instance, must avoid the risk of provoking laughter from the public. We must achieve a proper balance of elements in order to achieve harmony onstage." This involves assembling beautiful stage pictures, using the chorus as a mass ensemble, as in a painting. Sequi stresses that he does not want individuals to stand out, but rather a chorus used like expressive strokes in painting. In Romantic opera, the chorus is akin to a Greek chorus, conveying a single feeling, a single sentiment or expression as dictated by the composer at a particular moment.

Sequi recognizes the basic evanescence of these bel canto operas, with their exquisite music and old-fashioned drama. "The drama is not real," he insists, "so I don't intend to invent action or show what is *not* in the music. You can't go against the music, or you show up the fragility. You must go *with* the music. *Puritani* is not Pinter! For instance, in the wedding scene—a sublime moment—I made it like a *favola*, a children's fairy tale with a poetic atmosphere of the very old past, achieved through the groupings of the chorus and extras to approach early French Romantic paint-

ing. So this was a simple production—and simplicity is not easy."

His *I Puritani*, which to date has had but one "festival" run of performances, opens in Scene 1 with the impression of the sun rising, shafts of light illuminating the soldiers who sing in the delicate Bellini style. The scrims employed by Sequi and Lee are designed to make the action seem distant in time, the stage less grandly majestic. For Scene 2, a Gothic castle and church are merely suggested on an almost bare stage—a concept coming from Bellini's own time when all settings were painted flats, with no built pieces. Again, Sequi stresses the lack of realism in such a work and the overriding emphasis on personal feelings and subtle vocal inflections. Elvira conveys girlishness in her voice, just as Walton, her father, suggests age in his basso, both singers changing the expression to suit what lies in the music. For Elvira's mad scene, she is placed on Lee's broad staircase, alone, in the spotlight, the chorus dressed in subtle dark colors, because Sequi felt this scene akin to a movie close-up, the soprano's voice conveying the emotion inherent in her passion and her grief.

"Bel canto is a legitimate form of theater," Sequi believes, "with its conventions of arias, duets, trios, quartets, and concertati. You must understand the historical meaning of these conventions and accept them. The drama is expressed through the voice, like the poetic soliloquies in Shakespeare, in *Hamlet*. The magic of these moments gives the works their real quality. Yes, they are static, but the director cannot be contrary to what it really is. But always, it is *atmosphere*, the need for stage mood to help portray these characters' emotions."

Tannhäuser

WAGNER

Production: **Otto Schenk**   Sets: **Günther Schneider-Siemssen**
Costumes: **Patricia Zipprodt**   Lighting: **Gil Wechsler**

Tannhäuser

THE 1977 production of Wagner's *Tannhäuser*—directed by Otto Schenk and designed by Günther Schneider-Siemssen—was a revelation, for the simple reason that it set out onstage exactly what the composer had demanded when the work was first performed in 1845—but now presented in terms of modern, up-to-date, late-twentieth-century theater. One might even call this *Tannhäuser* a watershed staging, for in the cyclical fashions of theater style it marked a complete turnabout from the greatly abstracted versions of Wagner operas introduced by Wieland Wagner at Bayreuth in the 1950s and '60s, and then taken up by many theaters and many directors, among them Herbert von Karajan with his *Ring* cycle at Salzburg, later reproduced at the Met. Now there were no central discs, no rampant symbolism, no abstract projections, and for the singers the former statuesque placement and acting requirements were done away with. Straightforward realism in Wagner, as purveyed by the likes of Emil Preetorius in the 1930s, returned with full-blooded vengeance, and in a way that could demonstrate how effective such an approach can be in our own time.

The critics were unanimous in recognizing the important statement that Schenk and Schneider-Siemssen were making, for it conveyed a sense of magnificence and truth throughout. Rarely in recent years have a director and designer found such brilliant solutions in following almost to the letter the instructions set down by the composer-librettist. This honest, faithful staging showed that inspiration, beauty, and freshness could be applied in an ostensibly old-fashioned manner, but without becoming stuffy, dull or outmoded—as the previous Met staging had been. Schenk created the characters of Wagner's early opera by recognizing the work as a medieval fairy tale, but handling it with a totally modern acting style and commitment that made it dramatically viable, intense and clear-cut in its relationships. Schenk's brand of theater reaches back to the nineteenth century, and his success proves that there is room for such a style in our modern world. Schneider-Siemssen is Schenk's ideal collaborator as designer, for his work is filled with poetry and delicacy, showing an uncommon eye for the handling of color and vast spaces, and making good use of realistic projections on the broad rear cyclorama and scrims. The interior of the richly frescoed Italianate Wartburg Castle, flooded with sunlight and rich in atmosphere, is a burnished old-master canvas come to life, filled with Patricia Zipprodt's exquisite costumes in pastel-to-brilliant shades.

Schenk, long a celebrated actor in his native Austria, had worked at the Met previously, directing *Tosca* in 1968–69 and *Fidelio* in 1970–71. He was tackling *Tannhäuser* for the first time, although his designer had put his hand to it in Bremen several decades earlier. It was at the Bremen Stadttheater that Schneider-Siemssen launched his stage career, and he continued to work there from 1945 to 1962. After that he was invited by Karajan to become chief designer of the Vienna State Opera. Director and designer thus came to *Tannhäuser* fresh, with few preconceived ideas carried over from earlier productions. As Schenk told Leonie Rysanek, his leading lady, at the first rehearsal, "Yes, we all know that you are the greatest Elisabeth in the world, but now we are

Above
Günther Schneider-Siemssen's design for the wooded valley near the Wartburg, with pilgrims passing on their way to Rome; and (*right*) costume design for Wolfram by Patricia Zipprodt.

◁ *Overleaf*
Act II. The guests invited by the Landgrave Hermann (Fritz Hübner), who is accompanied by his niece Elisabeth (Eva Marton), enter the Wartburg for the singing contest. (*Inset*) Tannhäuser (James McCracken) shocks all present with his hymn to Venus.

going to start thinking of the role as if you were doing it for the first time." James Levine, too, had conducted the work only once before, and then in a concert version, so he also was approaching it with an open mind. The three men agreed that, as a product of Wagner's youth, *Tannhäuser* is directly in the mainstream of German Romantic opera, an immediate successor to Weber's *Der Freischütz*, for instance. The work therefore responds best to representational treatment that acknowledges its traditional grand-opera pageantry, as well as the human side of the drama.

Schenk said at the time, "The idea is to remake a period piece with our modern feelings, to retell an old story with new passion. It really took me a long time to see the essential simplicity of this opera. It is about a man caught in a mid-life crisis. The Minnesinger knight Tannhäuser, an actual figure of the Middle Ages, has spent a year living with the goddess Venus in the Venusberg, a hillside grotto that legend says is located in central Germany. His every sensual need is gratified, but he feels he must return to the real world to search for something intangible—call it spiritual fulfillment if you will. He returns to a strict 'establishment' society, a world of courtly behavior, but finds the environment narrow, conventional, stifling—even the 'pure' love of the reigning Landgrave's daughter, Elisabeth, is not enough for him. In the third act Venus returns to claim Tannhäuser just as Elisabeth dies praying for his salvation. The collision of these sacred and profane worlds literally destroys him. . . . Wagner's characters are incapable of compromise; they must be removed from their worlds through death. In a real sense this concept reflects Wagner's own struggles as an uncompromising artist. It also focuses on his personal problems in dealing with passion and love, a man who doesn't know where one starts and the other picks up. Where does one put the heart? This is not an invented Romantic notion, but an eternal struggle for everyone."

Overleaf ▷
Act II. In the minstrels' hall, the saintly Elisabeth (Leonie Rysanek) rejoices at the news of Tannhäuser's return— "Dich, teure Halle."
Act I (*inset*). The Venusberg, where revelers cavort in the grotto dwelling of the goddess of love.

Below
Act I, Scene 1. The minstrel Tannhäuser (James McCracken) sings in praise of Venus (Grace Bumbry), who reclines in sensual abandon.

Schenk came to realize that in this drama involving conflicting personalities, Tannhäuser's personal conflict exists within his own soul. As a director, Schenk's primary concern is the dramatic presence of his performers. He works on acting and characterization, not symbolic concepts, so that the drama arises not from scenic effects, but from the singers' facial expressions, their gestures, and their bodies. He was constantly urging this *Tannhäuser* cast toward greater subtlety, less obvious sentimentality—calling instead for those small touches that cumulatively add an extra dimension to the various characters they portray. During rehearsals Schenk began to strive for what he called "a love story between director and performer. It's all very well to work it out beforehand in discussion, but theater can only be created on the stage as the director senses the potential in each individual singer. A new production is like a beast that lies there and does not want to be bothered. My job is to tease the beast to life, make it do what I want until it strikes the audience as

formed energy. I want people to feel the fear and pity of Wagner's story and his music. To achieve this, a director must believe in the moment and not consciously look for solutions. Arbitrarily devised solutions and inventions kill the theater. Human behavior and passion form the essence of opera and drama."

Prior to this production of *Tannhäuser*, Schneider-Siemssen had worked in every conceivable style, including the darkly abstract for Karajan's *Ring* and other projects at Salzburg. As he observed, "*Tannhäuser* is not the cosmic sort of drama that *Tristan und Isolde* is, for instance. It is more earthy, and the stage picture must capture the mixture of old-fashioned grand opera with the new trends Wagner explores in his music. As in any stage design, the sets should run parallel with, and be translated from, the music. The countryside of Act I, Scene 1, for example, contains many elements of the actual landscape of Thuringia, the area of Germany where the action takes place. The stage is full of beech trees and the rolling hills one

Act I, Scene 2. Tannhäuser (James McCracken), standing by the wayside shrine, meets the Landgrave Hermann (John Macurdy) and his hunting party—Biterolf (Vern Shinall), Reinmar (John Cheek), Wolfram (Bernd Weikl), and Hermann, accompanied by two attendants.

finds in that part of the country. The same scene recurs in Act III, but now it is autumn, the leaves have fallen and now carpet the ground—all accomplished by light projections. For the great hall of the Wartburg in Act II, I used many authentic architectural details, columns and arches that still stand in the original castle. Instead of its rectangular dimensions, though, the room is oval in design, primarily for acoustical considerations, as well as facilitating the entrance march and assemblage of the song contestants."

Ultimately, this was no picture-postcard approach, for the team superbly conveyed the conflicts of spiritual and carnal love as represented by Elisabeth and Venus, the two opposites of medieval society which, despite their seemingly irreconcilable nature, Tannhäuser desires to synthesize. Due emphasis was also given to Wagner's allegorical view that the creative artist cannot live by the rules of a repressive society. Both aspects emerge as full-blooded human drama. The story may be a "once upon a time" fairy tale, but as Schenk noted, fairy tales can be very cruel, very human, and very Freudian. But one must not go too far in this direction either, or one risks killing the heart of the fairy tale. In considering the Paris edition used for this production (as opposed to the earlier, less sensual, Dresden edition), Schenk felt that a main problem lay in the abrupt changes in musical style: Tannhäuser's Rome Narrative in Act III, for instance, looks forward—anticipating the music of Strauss and Berg—while in other places, such as the final chorus of Act II, the style is *echt* nineteenth-century stand-up-and-sing Italian opera. As Schenk put it, "My job is to link these different musical ideas together with a thread of tension and passion so that the audience will believe in what is happening onstage."

The outcome of the approach adopted by director and designer is to imbue *Tannhäuser* with a vibrant sense of immediacy, of bridging a bygone world—actually two bygone worlds, one medieval, the other nineteenth-century (as suggested in the paintings of Caspar David Friedrich)—with our own contemporary theatrical sensibility. Lavish stage pictures seemed entirely appropriate to such a work, with its exact geographical locales as well as that important fairy-tale atmosphere. The misty, mossy Venusberg grotto immediately conveys a world of unbridled sensuality, with its languid lake and waterfall, its rocky niches for lovemaking, its phallic stalagmites and stalactites, and its arching ramp on which heated, writhing, sexual pursuits could be played out in Norbert Vesak's seductive choreography.

This escapist fantasy gave way in an instant (thanks to modern technology and projections) to the leafy hills and vale of the Wartburg—a

landscape featuring trees (albeit a touch stylized) about to burst into leaf, age-old rocky paths, and a primitive wooden wayside prayer shrine, all beneath an infinite blue sky. As one critic put it, you could almost smell the fresh earth and nature's rebirth in spring as the Shepherd piped his charming tune and Tannhäuser, kneeling in the same position as he had been only moments before with Venus, was greeted by his long-lost comrades who tell him of the song contest and Elisabeth.

In Act II, the interior of the Romanesque Wartburg spells tradition and traditional values, with its curved stone walls, ceiling frescoes rich in religious imagery, and wooden chairs and benches anchored to the floor. Through the arched opening to the rear center, from which light streams in, lies the unknown world beyond, and on a portico high above stand the eight heraldic trumpeters for the festivities of the song contest. With Gil Wechsler's sensitive lighting, the return to the hills for Act III immediately establishes a feeling of late autumn,

Act II. In the minstrels' hall of the Wartburg, Elisabeth (Leonie Rysanek) is comforted by her uncle, the Landgrave Hermann (John Macurdy).

The Act III finale: Tannhäuser
(James McCracken) lies dead
by the bier of Elisabeth
(Leonie Rysanek), as Wolfram
(Bernd Weikl) and Hermann
(John Macurdy) look on.

the ebbing of nature's annual cycle symbolized by fallen leaves, a murky sky (through which the planet Venus shines brightly, to be addressed by Wolfram), and bare branches—an ideal symbol for Elisabeth who must die in order to redeem the tormented, doomed minstrel who has found no salvation in his pilgrimage to the Pope in Rome. Elisabeth's long, slow exit after her prayer seems to lift her soul directly to heaven. The brief reappearance of Venus, far to stage rear, as she calls Tannhäuser back to her lotus-eating realm, is an impressive element in the mixture of these two worlds onstage, mirroring the conflict in Tannhäuser's own soul.

Like many other critics, Andrew Porter, writing in *The New Yorker*, hailed this bold return to ageless values in producing for the stage, calling it "a twentieth-century landmark in the history of Wagner staging," because of its commitment to doing Wagner as Wagner intended, abjuring any silly innovations or a bad imitation of the controversial Wieland Wagner style. Porter rejoiced in a public wanting "to see once again things that the music as well as the stage directions tell of: the beauty and grandeur of nature; human feelings revealed in a glance, a gesture . . .".

Porter saw that Schenk and Schneider-Siemssen adhered to the dictates of Wagner's pamphlet about producing the opera ("Über die Aufführung des *Tannhäuser*," dating from the late 1850s). The composer stresses the imitation of real life "in its noblest, freest forms," even in the Act II processional entry of the guests, during which each person is made to react in a characteristic manner on reentering this beloved Hall of Song after Tannhäuser's long-awaited return. Schenk's direction gave individuality to every member of the chorus, so that in the singing tournament each one reacted in a specific way to the course of events. Porter felt that the result remained fresh, lively, and faithful to the music and the drama. "This *Tannhäuser*," he wrote, "was never silly or stodgy or dated. In modernized treatments, the work can seem to be more than a creaking, long-winded, antiquated text for a dissertation upon varieties of human love, or an artist's social responsibility, or whatever. Here it would be enjoyed in all its richness as an exuberantly romantic grand opera in which a hundred different poetic, picturesque, and political ideas contribute to one lyrical and dramatic adventure."

Left and opposite

Act III. Wolfram (Bernd Weikl) calls upon the Evening Star to lead Elisabeth on her journey into heaven; and, exhausted after his visit to Rome, Tannhäuser (Richard Cassilly) describes to Wolfram how the Pope has rejected his plea for forgiveness.

Tristan und Isolde

IN EXPLAINING the concept of a hotly debated production of Wagner's *Tristan und Isolde* that originated at the Vienna State Opera in 1968 and was then adapted for the Met in 1971, the director August Everding noted in retrospect: ". . . it was a time of drugs, of getting away, of escaping, of the first man in space, of acid trips, of astrology. When the lovers drink the potion in Act I, that is their acid trip. It becomes a question of the change between reality and unreality, which is really the theme of the opera." When Everding made his debut at the Met in November 1971, it was as a result of a suggestion made by the Swedish soprano Birgit Nilsson, who had created his Isolde in Vienna. Everding and his designer, Günther Schneider-Siemssen, projected a haunting, other-worldly, poetic visualization of what Wagner had put into his score and text. Thus, the world of things and people is portrayed with literal realistic scenery and props that belong to one style of theater; but when hero and heroine drink the potion and fall in love, the realistic scenery vanishes and they find themselves afloat in a transfigured world of color, with abstract images reaching into infinity.

Scenic projections have long been a characteristic ingredient of Schneider-Siemssen's work, and here they are given a central role in creating limitless, mystical environments. He calls the technique "painting with light," and explains that "In a psychological drama such as *Tristan*, light speaks a stronger language than do props or fixed scenery. The sets are very spare. The ship, placed at an oblique angle, is 'real' until the potion takes effect. Then everything seems to dissolve until only the two lovers are visible—their environment means nothing. When Marke's contingent arrives, reality takes over again. Similarly, in the second act the lovers become isolated in their own dream, searching for love in infinity, in the eternal dark." By such means Wagner's whole poetic contrasting of light and dark, day and night, is translated into visual terms; no longer would an audience be made to feel uncomfortable while watching singers stiffly holding poses for virtual eternities while Wagner's conceptualized love music thunders forth. Instead, an overall tension is created in the gradual unfolding of the mythic love story.

Many critics felt that had Wagner had such sophisticated, almost cinematic, technical means at his disposal in the 1860s, he too would have traveled this route towards a visual realization of his erotic, philosophical *Tristan* drama. Certainly, one hears this flight from reality in the symphonic scoring, and his text alludes time and again to the reality of day versus the unreality of night. It is in this world of night—death—that the lovers must finally be united, their sexual communion at long last achieved as the famous Tristan chord is musically resolved. The work of Everding and Schneider-Siemssen was highly praised by Irving Kolodin in *The Saturday Review*: "It comes about as close to a perfect realization of what the composer himself called a *Gesamtkunstwerk*—a total work of art—as anything offered to the New York musical public in decades. It will remain, unquestionably, the outstanding scenic achievement of Sir Rudolf Bing's administration."

The heavy wooden vessel makes a magnificent spectacle when the curtain rises on Isolde and Brangäne in their quarters on board the ship that is carrying the Irish princess against her will to Cornwall. In the course of her furious narrative, with the indifferent Tristan very much in her mind, his proximity is graphically revealed on-stage; onto the set of billowing, square-cut sails above her quarters are thrown the shadows not only of the crew as they sing their sea song amid the ropes and ladders, but also that of the looming heroic figure of Tristan himself. This ominous shadow is to become an ever-present figure, seemingly set on a predetermined course in his voyage to eventual death—and in his unspoken acceptance of, and even yearning for, death. When Isolde fails to persuade the arrogant knight to come to her, she asks Brangäne to prepare a fatal potion for the man who killed her fiancé Morold and who has since betrayed her by taking her to his own land as a bride for his uncle, King Marke. In fact, Tristan and Isolde have merged mentally and emotionally long before the moment when finally—with land in sight—they share what has become a "love potion," a drink that serves simply

Above

Director August Everding discusses the role of Tristan with Jess Thomas; and (*right*) Günther Schneider-Siemssen, who also designed the Met's productions of *Tannhäuser* and *Les Contes d'Hoffmann.*

◁ *Overleaf*

Act I. Tristan (Jess Thomas) and Isolde (Birgit Nilsson) drink the love potion which she believes to be poison.

each other, transported to another plane of existence—only to be brought back to harsh reality by the landing of the ship and the arrival on board of Marke and his party. Reality takes over again: brilliant gold court costumes and pageantry fill the stage, and the ship and its mighty sails are restored to their original aspect. The act ends with Isolde—enveloped in her voluminous cape—falling in a faint as the curtain descends amid orchestral fanfare—all to powerful and chilling effect. In these final moments of Act I, Everding portrays the couple's outward loyalties, morality, and obligations in collision with their love for each other, and this is expressed in thrilling unison by music, text, physical action, and visual effects. "In their world," observes Everding, "there is no morality, no laws. It could be Beckett."

Overleaf ▷
Act I. As Isolde (Birgit Nilsson) is borne by ship to Cornwall to marry King Marke, the shadow of Tristan, who has betrayed her, looms on a mighty sail.
(*Inset*) Isolde, in revenge, commands her companion Brangäne (Mignon Dunn) to prepare a poison draught for Tristan and herself.

Left and below
Act I. The attendants of Tristan and Isolde: Kurwenal (Donald McIntyre) and Brangäne (Tatiana Troyanos).

to externalize and bring to the surface the feelings each has long felt for the other; and the love thus released asserts itself in overcoming the loyalties and obligations by which they have been long constrained.

With the help of the stage-center elevator, and with the stage plunged into darkness except for pinpoint spotlights on their faces and their hands clutching the goblet, the mute pair rise slowly into limitless space, into the galaxies, far from their earthly surroundings, entering—as it were—a kind of celestial orbit in which they are inextricably bound forever. As the orchestra sings of their newly awakened love, of the liberation of their repressed emotions, they become hypnotized by

Tristan und Isolde 227

The intermingling of reality and ideal remoteness is extended in the lengthy second act. Isolde waits with Brangäne on a wide stone terrace to stage right as Marke's hunting party recedes into the forest. The set for the moonlit castle gardens depicts a maze of leafy trees, where the princess finally greets her knight, and in their love duet they begin once again to ascend to their own private world, this vision of romantic wonderland as mirrored in Wagner's searching music. The seated couple slowly transcend their surroundings as they soar toward the heavens; at one moment they are silhouetted against a vast expanse of water under a cloud-swirled sky in which large clusters of stars seem to sparkle like diamonds. As they ascend higher and higher, appearing to float on the curved edge of the world, great cosmic starbursts and comets are seen coming and going in the galaxies. The production team conceived the duet as a cinematic progression of mystery-laden dissolves, close-ups, fade-ins, and fade-outs while the couple float ecstatically in space, oblivious to the rest of the world. As Brangäne stands high above the stage, totally removed from the world, her warning seems to float upward on the air to the unheeding lovers. Perhaps it was the 1960s fascination with

outer space and the first moon landing that made this concept seem so immediate, striking, and appropriate.

But with the abrupt return of King Marke and his retinue, the lovers are again plunged into reality and suddenly exposed, the garden turns a dark wintry gray, the now leafless trees symbolically reflecting the bleakness of the music. Tristan's haunted, inherent longing for death is strongly realized as he is wounded by Melot's sword—if he is to forgo the celestial ecstasy he has just experienced with Isolde, death is the only alternative.

Above
Aage Haugland as Marke.

Overleaf ▷
Act II. Isolde (Birgit Nilsson) and Tristan (Jess Thomas) transfigured in their night of love (*left*). Tristan (Richard Cassilly), brought back to reality by the unexpected appearance of King Marke, seeks reassurance (*above, right*) from Isolde (Hildegard Behrens) that she will follow him—even unto death. Act III. (*Below, right*) Isolde (Birgit Nilsson) stands by the body of Tristan (Jess Thomas)—the Liebestod.

Tristan und Isolde   231

Act III. In Brittany, Tristan (Jess Thomas) lies fatally wounded; with him are the faithful Kurwenal (Thomas Stewart), and the Shepherd (Nico Castel).

Tristan's delirium in Act III prompts not so much a feeling of a real place at Kareol, his home in Brittany, as an abstracted semicircular stone wall, on which the lonely Shepherd can sit as he plays his mournful pipes. With a bleak but glaring winter sun beating down on the dying, agonizing, hallucinating Tristan, Schneider-Siemssen creates a confined, hopeless arena for death. At the height of his frightening delirium, as he waits for Isolde to arrive, Tristan marshals his last ounce of strength in a desperate attempt to scale the wall, to escape from an all-confining world, but there is no escape except in death. As his lover arrives, he utters his unbearably poignant "Isolde!", and at the end the lovers find eternal union free of all earthly concerns. The transfigured Isolde ascends to the cosmos, where her soul will be joined with Tristan's.

If Schneider-Siemssen shows a strong affinity for the works of Wagner, it may be because, as a student in Munich during the Clemens Krauss era, he served as an apprentice in scenery-painting at the Bavarian State Opera and later studied with Emil Preetorius at the Munich Academy; one often feels the influence of that major Bayreuth artist of the 1930s on his work. Like several other leading figures in the world of opera, Everding came to the lyric theater by way of the legitimate theater. A constant source of fascination to him has been the contrast between what is real and what is fantasy, imaginary, surreal or mythic. "You must listen to the music," he declares. "You have to follow the music to interpret a work. My job is to stage an opera—not make a social comment . . . You have to have the time to tell the singers how to fall, how to react, all these things. Coming from the straight theater, I know that this must be done with psychological insight. For me it's very important to have human beings onstage, acting and reacting."

Everding has admitted that at first he did not like working in opera (especially as compared with doing new plays), because of the elements of unnatural behavior and artificiality inherent in opera. "When Böhm asked me to do *Tristan* in Vienna," he says, "my relationship with Wagner's music was a negative one. I was born in 1928, and I grew up in the time of Hitler, when Wagner's music was misused and abused. I felt distant from it and really hated it. It made a tremendous change in my life to undertake *Tristan*. I studied it and discovered what genius is there. I ended up feeling that but for Wagner we would not have modern music."

Since that 1967 beginning, Everding has staged new *Tristan* productions at Bayreuth and Munich, both dramatically different from his first concep-tion. "A production," he insists, "is of a definite period. There is no absolute truth in the thea-ter—only what is right for a few years. So an opera presents a challenge every time we do it. In the theater, I never do the same play twice, but an opera I may do four or five times, and each time I approach it differently. Productions age tremen-dously in eight or ten years. Then they are finished."

Over the years, in subsequent Met revivals, Everding did substantially reduce the original psychedelic effects of this *Tristan*. But his favorite recollection of the production—with Birgit Nils-son and Jess Thomas in the title roles—concerns the lighting: "I was yelling that I needed two stars in the sky, and Bing said, 'You don't need two stars—you have two onstage.' "

Act III. Kurwenal (Thomas Stewart) comes to the aid of the wounded Tristan (Jess Thomas).

Die Zauberflöte

MOZART

Production: **Günther Rennert**
Sets and Costumes: **Marc Chagall**

Left
After the dress rehearsal, a moment of relaxation: Pilar Lorengar (Pamina), Hermann Prey (Papageno), designer Marc Chagall, who died in March 1985, director Günther Rennert, Lucia Popp (Queen of the Night), and conductor Josef Krips.

Die Zauberflöte

Opposite
Act I, Scene 1. The Queen of the Night (Roberta Peters) asks the bewildered Tamino (George Shirley) to rescue her daughter from "evil captors."

◁ Overleaf
Tamino (Nicolai Gedda) tames wild animals with his magic flute.

NOWADAYS it has become rare for celebrated painters to work in the theater. In the early part of this century, however, the dynamic impresario of the Ballets Russes, Sergei Diaghilev, commissioned many of the leading visual artists of his time and lifted their collaborative efforts with composers, writers, and performers to unprecedented heights. It was the historical resonances of his achievements that were sounded when Rudolf Bing invited the Russian-born painter Marc Chagall to design the sets and costumes for a new German-language production—the first at the Met for forty years—of Mozart's *Die Zauberflöte*, which was to enter the repertory in the company's first season in its new home at Lincoln Center, 1966–67. For Chagall, who had never designed an opera, this was to become an extraordinary event, particularly since he would be dealing with his favorite among the operas of Mozart, a composer he had long adored. The results were sophisticated, whimsical, and highly personal.

At the same time, the Met had commissioned the artist to paint two gigantic murals for the front panels of the new edifice designed by Wallace K. Harrison, and his yellow-dominated "The Sources of Music" and red-dominated "The Triumph of Music"—with their myriad references to Orpheus, Beethoven, Wagner, Mozart and *The Magic Flute* (including a red Papageno with his pan pipes and basket of birds), Verdi, New York, the Ballet, the Firebird, French music, Russian music and Chagall himself—were installed on the Grand Tier foyer level. Indeed, these murals can be seen as an extension of, or an epilogue to, Chagall's work on the Mozart opera, since the two projects—both executed in the artist's inimitable style— in fact complement one another.

By the 1960s, Chagall was already one of the legendary figures of twentieth-century art, and in fact he had previously designed for the theater in New York in the 1940s: *Aleko* and *The Firebird* for the Ballet Theater. (His *Firebird* later became a staple of the New York City Ballet.) Historically, there was also a direct connection with Diaghilev, for Chagall's first contact with the theater went back to 1909 when he studied scenery painting in the St. Petersburg studio of Léon Bakst, who just a year later became one of Diaghilev's chief designers—and who considered the Ballets Russes to be not yet ready for Chagall's advanced theories about decor.

It was that link of artist and stage that was reforged when Chagall agreed to his old friend Bing's proposal that he design *Die Zauberflöte*. (As a youngster in Vienna, Bing had fallen in love with Chagall's childlike magic world, and the two men had a close personal link through their wives—Chagall's second wife Vava being a close friend of Nina Bing's since their schooldays.) When Bing began to plan his first season in the new house, he felt that Chagall's fantasy world would provide just the right foil for and complement to Mozart's magic, an opinion heartily endorsed by the veteran Günther Rennert, who had been engaged to direct the production.

A painter's visual world and that enclosed by the

proscenium arch are not always compatible. Chagall's innocent vision, as in his early Russian paintings, features swirling phantasmagorias of flying animals and floating, soaring figures joined in space by brilliant color—hardly the world of real, earthbound people. The human form and its capabilities give the stage its sense of order—and impose its limitations—whereas Chagall once declared that for him a picture is a surface bearing representations in which logic and illustration have no importance. The visual effect of his composition is what he feels to be of prime importance.

There were critics who considered that Chagall's style simply drowned or smothered the subject and music of Mozart's opera. In his concept of *Die Zauberflöte*, the elements of Chagall's familiar imagery, so closely associated with his own background, actually have little to do with the characters and setting of Emanuel Schikaneder's libretto. As art critic Emily Genauer saw it, "In *The Magic Flute* the figures who have so long inhabited Chagall's world of fantasy become, strangely, almost abstractions, enormously inventive allegorical embodiments of the love and joy of life, the sense of mystery, the victory of good over evil, the nobility and the solemn aspiration which are in Mozart's music."

Color—and unity through color—is the key to Chagall's later works, and never more so than in his vast designs for *Die Zauberflöte*, in which brilliant hues, from one end of the spectrum to the other, are juxtaposed. Basically, Chagall responded to what he heard in the music. In fact, he prepared all his designs while listening to the music. Even so, the results suggested no literal reading of Schikaneder's often chaotic and inconsistent libretto, since the artist found this fairy tale a childlike, complex mélange. For him the characters had to be viewed as abstractions: Sarastro as a symbol of light, reason, eternity, wisdom; the Queen of the Night as vengeance and destructiveness; Monostatos as treason and lechery; Papageno as an embodiment of materialism, in the simple, healthy longing for good food and a loving wife; Tamino as idealism. The opera is concerned with the ultimate victory of wisdom over ignorance, truth over treachery, experience over innocence. Little attention was paid to the element of Freemasonry, since Chagall saw it as symptomatic of a kind of general religiosity prevalent in Mozart's time, but not of the eternal values symbolized in the opera. Nor did he set the work in the prescribed Egypt. Since he did not regard the pyramids as being Egyptian *per se* but rather as representing, in the philosophy of Freemasonry, the highest truth in life, he created his own version—no more than vague triangles, their peaks symbolizing the highest wisdom.

Above
The Three Ladies (Rosalind Elias, Jean Fenn, and Ruza Pospinov-Baldani) admire the handsome Tamino (Nicolai Gedda), who has fainted at the sight of a giant serpent.

Left
Design by Chagall for a drop curtain seen during the overture.

Right
Papageno (Theodor Uppman), with his enchanted bells.

Opposite

Act II, Scene 5. The Genii (Cynthia Munzer, Betsy Norden, and Christine Weidinger) return to calm Pamina (Benita Valente) and prevent her from using a dagger to take her own life.

Below

Act I, Scene 3. In Sarastro's realm, Papageno (Christian Boesch), with Pamina (Leona Mitchell), uses his magic bells to subdue the threatening actions of Monostatos (James Atherton) and his slaves.

The artist's approach became more abstract, more generalized, since he felt that we need only read between the lines of the libretto in order to see the many levels of meaning. He noted that Mozart never did anything simply for effect, that in his compositions every detail has a precise place. In this way, Chagall tried to express a large conception, subordinating details to that main idea and to the logic of the structure. Rational explanation was not at the core of his thinking—he felt that nature should be seen as abstract, beyond rational explanation, What he viewed as a feature common to himself and to Mozart was the "celebration of the sweetness of nature," and through his painting he sought to depict this. "I paint demons, grotesque little animals, all sorts of unreal creatures I have invented. They are symbols, masks to conceal the sordid faces of the world, delimiting and shutting out what is evil. I focus on gladness and joy. I use my art as eyeglasses through which I can see only what is good and beautiful and true. I offer my art as spectacles to others, so they also can see my vision of the world, the joy of living. Mozart did the same thing."

Particularly in the scenes with animals, the familiar Chagall figures are in evidence. The magic flute transforms these animals, enchanting them into a state of wonderment, as art shows its power to tame wild beasts. The same is true of Chagall's half-man-half-bird Papageno and the smoke-breathing serpent—in the form of a big, cuddly, bloated worm with eight eyes and the initials "M.C." on its ear—killed by the Three Ladies in Scene 1. The world of Chagall's *Die Zauberflöte* is

replete with Genii who magically materialize, disappearing princesses, sorcerers, bearded patriarchs, and a comic figure with magic bells, together with a menagerie of snakes, birds, fish, horses, and cows. This is not reality, only Chagall's imaginative world of light and color. As well as the vague triangles representing pyramids, he also created great whirling discs for the Temple of the Sun, and veiled, mysterious places for caves in which to hold the trials by fire and water. As Emily Genauer concluded, "The result is a world of illusion, of dream, of fantasy, where color, line, and shape are fused with each other and with the music to create the only reality, beauty, and love,

which Chagall recognizes and which he believes was also Mozart's only reality."

In all, Chagall realized—in what proved to be a grand one-man show—thirteen full curtains, each about seventy feet tall and forty feet wide, plus twenty-six additional partial curtains (side pieces) and 121 costumes. The side pieces, with their vivid colors, add still more depictions of animals, people, and demons, while his costumes texturally fit into the overall theatrical concept. The result is a grandiose theater of design, an eye-filling spectacle in which the singers often become absorbed into the totality, rather than standing out in relief, as in most opera productions.

Overleaf ▷

In the finale, Tamino (Stuart Burrows) and Pamina (Adriana Maliponte) are united by Sarastro (Hans Sotin), as the populace extol the victory of courage and wisdom. The inset shows the previous scene—the Queen of the Night (Edda Moser) with the Second Lady (Mildred Miller) and Monostatos (Paul Franke)—in which the powers of darkness are finally defeated.

Opposite
Act II, Scene 10. Tamino
(David Kuebler) and Pamina
(Kathleen Battle), united by
the high priest Sarastro
(Martti Talvela).

Below
Act II, Scene 8. Papageno
(Theodor Uppman) is reunited
with Papagena (Patricia
Welting), and together they
rejoice at the prospect of
having their own brood of
bird-children.

For this staging of *Die Zauberflöte* the Met enjoyed the services of one of the finest of German stage directors of the day, Günther Rennert, whose visionary qualities also made a substantial contribution to the success of the production. Born in Essen in 1911, Rennert grew up in the heyday of Max Reinhardt, Heinz Tietjen, Jürgen Feling, Gustaf Gründgens, and Lothar Wallerstein—men who brought new prominence to the role of the stage director. As a young man, he was an apprentice of the legendary Walter Felsenstein before striking out on his own, in the years following World War II, in theater and opera. Through his work in Berlin, Hamburg, Munich, and at Glyndebourne, together with guest appearances elsewhere, Rennert established his personal objective: to reach an audience that will accept music as a medium of communication, a carrier and transmitter of ideas and content. At the time of his Met *Zauberflöte*, he had become general manager and resident director of the Bavarian State Opera, and shortly before his death in 1978,

he philosophized: "Neither music, the phenomenon of the human voice, the plot nor the ideas expressed in a libretto are by themselves the source of opera's fascination. No, the secret of this timeless impact is deliberate unreality. We build an unreal world of allegory, which by its transcendental magic gains the validity it seemingly loses. An opera is not a play with musical accompaniment: music gives the words a new, enhanced dimension toward the realm of magical unreality." And it was this magical unreality that he achieved with this *Zauberflöte*, bringing out the allegorical aspects, solemnity and nobility, frolic and fun, mystery and wonder. He was also immensely helped by the conducting of Josef Krips and by a superb cast of principals: Pilar Lorengar, Lucia Popp, Nicolai Gedda, Hermann Prey, and Jerome Hines. Indeed, the successful fusion of all the various elements of planning, execution, music-making, and design gave the world one of its most individual and successful conceptions since the innovative halcyon years of Diaghilev.

Performance history

COMPILED BY JEAN UPPMAN

La Bohème

PUCCINI

Production by **Franco Zeffirelli**
Sets designed by **Franco Zeffirelli**
Costumes designed by **Peter J. Hall**
Lighting designed by **Gil Wechsler**
Premiere: December 14, 1981
Production a gift of Mrs. Donald D. Harrington

Mimi: Teresa Stratas/Linda Zoghby/Teresa Zylis-Gara/Natalia Rom/ Catherine Malfitano/Mirella Freni/Ileana Cotrubas/Rosario Andrade/Eugenia Moldoveanu

Rodolfo: José Carreras/Ermanno Mauro/Giuliano Ciannella/Placido Domingo/Vasile Moldoveanu/Dano Raffanti/Neil Shicoff/Enrico Di Giuseppe/Luis Lima

Musetta: Renata Scotto/Julia Migenes-Johnson/Patricia Craig/ Carol Neblett/Myra Merritt/Barbara Daniels/Marilyn Zschau

Marcello: Richard Stilwell/Ryan Edwards/Brent Ellis/Brian Schexnayder/Pablo Elvira

Schaunard: Allan Monk/Mario Sereni/Darren Nimnicht/Vernon Hartman/Allan Glassman

Colline: James Morris/Julien Robbins/Paul Plishka/Richard Vernon/ John Cheek

Benoit: Italo Tajo/Renato Capecchi/Ara Berberian

Alcindoro: Italo Tajo/Renato Capecchi/Ara Berberian

Parpignol: Dale Caldwell/John Hanriot/John Bills/Arthur Apy

Sergeant: Glen Bater/Frank Coffey/Domenico Simeone/Peter Sliker/Vladimir Chistiakov/Paul De Paola

Officer: James Brewer/Talmadge Harper/Herman Marcus/Donald Peck/Edward Ghazal/Sven Leaf

Conductors: James Levine/Jeffrey Tate/Eugene Kohn/Placido Domingo

Boris Godunov

MUSSORGSKY

Production by **August Everding**
Sets designed by **Ming Cho Lee**
Costumes designed by **Peter J. Hall**
Choreography by **George Balanchine**
Premiere: December 16, 1974
Production a gift of Mrs. DeWitt Wallace

Boris: Martti Talvela/Jerome Hines/John Macurdy/Aage Haugland/ Paul Plishka/Sergei Kopchak

Shouisky: Robert Nagy/Andrea Velis/Charles Anthony/John Gilmore

Pimen: Paul Plishka/John Macurdy/Richard T. Gill/John Cheek/ Donald Gramm/Richard Vernon

Grigory: Harry Theyard/William Lewis/Misha Raitzin/Wieslaw Ochman

Marina: Mignon Dunn/Klara Barlow/Florence Quivar/Nedda Casei/ Gwynn Cornell/Stefka Mineva

Rangoni: William Dooley/Morley Meredith/Vern Shinall/John Darrenkamp

Varlaam: Donald Gramm/Raymond Michalski/Fernando Corena/ Marius Rintzler/Paul Plishka/Ara Berberian

Simpleton: Andrea Velis/Nico Castel/Robert Schmorr/James Atherton/Misha Raitzin

Nikitich: Andrij Dobriansky

Mitiukh: Edmond Karlsrud/Philip Booth/James Courtney

Shchelkalov: Lenus Carlson/Arthur Thompson/Allan Monk/ Richard Fredricks

Innkeeper: Batyah Godfrey/Shirley Love/Geraldine Decker

Missail: Paul Franke/Charles Anthony/Nico Castel

Officer: Richard Best/William Fleck/Andrij Dobriansky

Ksenia: Betsy Norden/Loretta Di Franco/Louise Wohlafka/Marvis Martin

Feodor: Paul Offenkrantz/Paul La Medica/Robert Sapolsky/Charlie Coleman

Nurse: Cynthia Munzer/Shirley Love/Batyah Godfrey/Ariel Bybee/ Geraldine Decker

Khrushchov: Robert Schmorr/Luigi Marcella/Charles Kuestner/ Emil Filip

Lavitsky: Robert Goodloe/Vladimir Chistiakov/Gene Boucher/ Darren Nimnicht

Chernikovsky: Charles Anthony/William Mellow/John Carpenter/ Anthony Laciura/David Kneuss

Boyar in attendance: Robert Schmorr/Luigi Marcella/Charles Kuestner/Emil Filip

Conductors: Thomas Schippers/Kazimierz Kord/Richard Woitach/ James Conlon

Cavalleria Rusticana/Pagliacci

MASCAGNI/LEONCAVALLO

Production by **Franco Zeffirelli**
Designed by **Franco Zeffirelli**
Premiere: January 8, 1970
Production a gift of the Glen Alden Foundation

Cavalleria Rusticana

Santuzza: Grace Bumbry/Ina Delcampo/Marie Collier/Fiorenza Cossotto/Martina Arroya/Irene Dalis/Elinor Ross/Regine Crespin/ Rita Hunter/Joann Grillo/Mignon Dunn/Tatiana Troyanos/ Bianca Berini/Bruna Baglioni/Galina Savova

Turiddu: Franco Corelli/Franco Tagliavini/Richard Tucker/Enrico Di Giuseppe/Placido Domingo/Sándor Kónya/Carlo Bergonzi/ Barry Morell/Harry Theyard/William Lewis/Wieslaw Ochman/ Anatoly Solovianenko/Gianfranco Cecchele/Juan Lloveras/Carlo Bini/Herman Malamood/Ermanno Mauro

Lola: Nedda Casei/Judith Forst/Joann Grillo/Frederica Von Stade/ Mildred Miller/Marcia Baldwin/Shirley Love/Isola Jones

Alfio: Frank Guarrera/Walter Cassel/Morley Meredith/Anselmo Colzani/Matteo Manuguerra/Guillermo Sarabia/Cornell MacNeil/Vern Shinall/Mario Sereni/Pablo Elvira/Ryan Edwards

Lucia: Carlotta Ordassy/Jean Kraft/Batyah Godfrey/Geraldine Decker

Conductors: Leonard Bernstein/Kurt Adler/Fausto Cleva/Christopher Keene/Carlo Felice Cillario/John Nelson/Giuseppe Patanè/Richard Woitach/James Levine/Michelangelo Veltri/David Stivender

Pagliacci

Nedda: Lucine Amara/Teresa Stratas/Jeannette Pilou/Edda Moser/Raina Kabaivanska/Gilda Cruz-Romo/Maria Bieshu/Lilian Sukis/Atsuko Azuma/Anna Moffo/Elena Mauti-Nunziata/Maralin Niska/Mariana Niculescu/Catherine Malfitano/Patricia Craig/Julia Migenes-Johnson

Canio: Richard Tucker/James McCracken/Robert Nagy/Josef Gabriels/Ludovic Spiess/Jon Vickers/Ermanno Mauro/Giuseppe Giacomini/Placido Domingo/Carlo Bergonzi/Richard Cassilly/Herman Malamood

Tonio: Sherrill Milnes/Frank Guarrera/Cornell MacNeil/Mario Sereni/Norman Mittelmann/Anselmo Colzani/Louis Quilico/Pablo Elvira

Silvio: William Walker/Dominic Cossa/Russell Christopher/Raymond Gibbs/Theodor Uppman/Lenus Carlson/Thomas Palmer/Ryan Edwards/Allan Monk/Dale Duesing/Brent Ellis/Brian Schexnayder/Arthur Thompson

Beppe: Andrea Velis/Robert Schmorr/James Atherton/Philip Creech

Villagers: William Mellow/Paul De Paola/Fawayne Murphy/Frank Coffey/Peter Sliker/Richard Firmin/Erbert Aldridge/Glen Bater/Arthur Apy/Domenico Simeone/Robert Kelly/Robert Manno/Dale Caldwell/Edward Ghazal/Emil Filip

Conductors: Fausto Cleva/Kurt Adler/Christopher Keene/Carlo Felice Cillario/John Nelson/Giuseppe Patanè/Richard Woitach/James Levine/Michelangelo Veltri/David Stivender

Les Contes d'Hoffmann
OFFENBACH

Production by **Otto Schenk**
Sets designed by **Günther Schneider-Siemssen**
Costumes designed by **Gaby Frey**
Lighting designed by **Gil Wechsler**
Premiere: March 8, 1982
Production a gift of Francis Goelet, Laurence D. Lovett, and the Metropolitan Opera Guild

Hoffmann: Placido Domingo/Kenneth Riegel/John Alexander/Neil Shicoff/William Lewis/Alfredo Kraus

Olympia: Ruth Welting/Gwendolyn Bradley/Gianna Rolandi/Catherine Malfitano

Giulietta: Tatiana Troyanos/Viorica Cortez/Isola Jones/Catherine Malfitano

Antonia: Christiane Eda-Pierre/Catherine Malfitano/Rosario Andrade/Myra Merritt

Stella: Pauline Andrey/Catherine Malfitano

Lindorf: Michael Devlin/James Morris/Richard Fredricks

Coppélius: Michael Devlin/James Morris/Richard Fredricks

Dappertutto: Michael Devlin/James Morris/Richard Fredricks

Nicklausse: Anne Howells/Ariel Bybee/Claudia Catania

Miracle: Michael Devlin/James Morris/Richard Fredricks

Muse: Anne Howells/Ariel Bybee/Claudia Catania

Andrès: Michel Sénéchal/James Atherton/Andrea Velis/Anthony Laciura

Cochénille: Michel Sénéchal/James Atherton/Andrea Velis/Anthony Laciura

Pitichinaccio: Michel Sénéchal/James Atherton/Andrea Velis/Anthony Laciura

Frantz: Michel Sénéchal/James Atherton/Andrea Velis/Anthony Laciura

Luther: William Fleck/Andrij Dobriansky

Nathanael: Michael Best/Charles Anthony

Hermann: John Darrenkamp/David Bernard

Spalanzani: Andrea Velis/Nico Castel/Anthony Laciura

Schlémil: Morley Meredith

Crespel: John Macurdy/Ara Berberian

Mother's Voice: Jean Kraft/Lili Chookasian/Hillary Johnsson

Conductors: Riccardo Chailly/Julius Rudel

Falstaff
VERDI

Production by **Franco Zeffirelli**
Designed by **Franco Zeffirelli**
Premiere: March 6, 1964
Production a gift of Mrs. John D. Rockefeller, Jr.

Falstaff: Anselmo Colzani/Fernando Corena/Geraint Evans/Ezio Flagello/Tito Gobbi/Cornell MacNeil

Alice: Gabriella Tucci/Raina Kabaivanska/Mary Curtis-Verna/Mary Costa/Pilar Lorengar/Phyllis Curtin/Renata Tebaldi/Lucine Amara/Evelyn Lear

Ford: Mario Sereni/Frank Guarrera/Thomas Stewart/Kostas Paskalis/Matteo Manuguerra/William Walker

Quickly: Regina Resnik/Lili Chookasian/Fedora Barbieri

Nannetta: Judith Raskin/Jeanette Scovotti/Mary Ellen Pracht Jeannette Pilou/Judith Blegen/Roberta Peters/Benita Valente

Fenton: Luigi Alva/George Shirley/Douglas Ahlstedt/Enrico Di Giuseppe

Meg: Rosalind Elias/Marcia Baldwin/Mildred Miller/Joann Grillo

Cajus: Paul Franke/Mariano Caruso

Bardolfo: Andrea Velis

Pistola: Norman Scott/Agostino Ferrin/Richard Best/Andrij Dobriansky

Mistress of the Inn: Rae Calitri/Lorraine Calcagno

Innkeeper: Thomas Powell

Conductors: Leonard Bernstein/Martin Rich/Joseph Rosenstock/Bruno Amaducci/Christoph Von Dohnanyi/James Levine/Peter Maag

Fidelio
BEETHOVEN

Production by **Otto Schenk**
Designed by **Boris Aronson**
Premiere: December 16, 1970
Production a gift of Mrs. John D. Rockefeller, Jr.

Leonore: Leonie Rysanek/Hildegard Hillebrecht/Klara Barlow/
Christa Ludwig/Caterina Ligendza/Ingrid Bjoner/Anja Silja/
Gwyneth Jones/Rose Wagemann/Hildegard Behrens/Shirley
Verrett/Johanna Meier/Eva Marton

Florestan: Jon Vickers/Robert Nagy/Helge Brilioth/James
McCracken/Jess Thomas/James King/Edward Sooter

Pizarro: Walter Berry/William Dooley/Morley Meredith/Donald
McIntyre/Siegmund Nimsgern/Franz Ferdinand Nentwig/Leif
Roar/Franz Mazura

Rocco: Giorgio Tozzi/John Macurdy/Kurt Moll/Paul Plishka/
William Wildermann/Matti Salminen

Marzelline: Judith Blegen/Edith Mathis/Judith Raskin/Joy
Clements/Christine Weidinger/Arleen Auger/Roberta Peters/
Catherine Malfitano/Elizabeth Volkman/Eleanor Bergquist

Jacquino: Murray Dickie/Leo Goeke/Kenneth Riegel/James
Atherton/Jon Garrison/Michael Best

Fernando: John Macurdy/Edmond Karlsrud/Paul Plishka/James
Morris/Philip Booth/Bernd Weikl/John Cheek/Julien Robbins/
Aage Haugland

Prisoners: Leo Goeke/Clifford Harvuot/Rod MacWherter/Paul
Franke/Robert Schmorr/Russell Christopher/Nico Castel/Edmond
Karlsrud/Raymond Gibbs/Douglas Ahlstedt/Arthur Thompson/
John Carpenter/Timothy Jenkins/Dana Talley/Charles Anthony/
Norman Andersson/Anthony Laciura/James Courtney

Captain: Harold Sternberg

Conductors: Karl Böhm/Hans Wallat/John Mauceri/Erich
Leinsdorf/Bernard Haitink/Klaus Tennstedt

Francesca da Rimini
ZANDONAI

Production by **Piero Faggioni**
Sets designed by **Ezio Frigerio**
Costumes designed by **Franca Squarciapino**
Lighting designed by **Gil Wechsler**
Premiere: March 9, 1984
Production a gift of Mrs. Donald D. Harrington

Francesca: Renata Scotto/Nicole Lorange

Paolo: Placido Domingo

Giovanni ("Gianciotto"): Cornell MacNeil/Richard J. Clark

Malatestino: William Lewis

Samaritana: Nicole Lorange/Loretta Di Franco

Smaragdi: Isola Jones

Garsenda: Gail Robinson/Myra Merritt

Biancofiore: Natalia Rom

Altichiara: Gail Dubinbaum/Lucille Beer

Donella: Claudia Catania

Simonetto: Brian Schexnayder/Allan Glassman

Ostasio: Richard Fredricks/Vernon Hartman

Toldo: Anthony Laciura

Berlingerio: John Darrenkamp

Archer: John Gilmore/Paul Franke

Prisoner: John Bills/Kun Yul Yoo

Conductor: James Levine

Die Frau ohne Schatten
STRAUSS

Production by **Nathaniel Merrill**
Designed by **Robert O'Hearn**
Choreography by **William Burdick**
Premiere: October 2, 1966
Production a gift in memory of Mrs. Izaak Walton Killam

Empress: Leonie Rysanek/Ingrid Bjoner/Eva Marton

Emperor: James King/Robert Nagy/Gerd Brenneis

Dyer's Wife: Christa Ludwig/Inge Borkh/Ursula Schröder-Feinen/
Birgit Nilsson/Brenda Roberts

Barak (Dyer): Walter Berry/Franz Ferdinand Nentwig

Nurse: Irene Dalis/Mignon Dunn/Gwynn Cornell

Messenger: William Dooley/Vern Shinall/Franz Mazura

Falcon: Carlotta Ordassy/Louise Wohlafka

Hunchback: Paul Franke/John Gilmore

One-Eyed: Clifford Harvuot/Theodore Lambrinos/Russell
Christopher

One-Armed: Lorenzo Alvary/James Courtney

Servants: Loretta Di Franco/Karan Armstrong/Nancy Williams/
Judith Forst/Carol Wilcox/Ivanka Myhal/Alma Jean Smith/Ariel
Bybee/Isola Jones/Gwendolyn Bradley/Therese Brandson

Apparition: Robert Nagy/Rod MacWherter/John Carpenter/
Timothy Jenkins

Unborn: Patricia Welting/Margaret Kalil/Marcia Baldwin/Joann
Grillo/Shirley Love/Lilian Sukis/Loretta Di Franco/Mary Fercana/
Karan Armstrong/Nedda Casei/Raeschele Potter/Frederica Von
Stade/Judith De Paul/Ann Florio/Betsy Norden/Alma Jean
Smith/Isola Jones/Jean Kraft/Ariel Bybee/Elinor Harper/Therese
Brandson/Claudia Catania

Watchmen: Charles Anthony/Robert Goodloe/Russell Christopher/
Gene Boucher/Leo Goeke/Raymond Gibbs/Robert Schmorr/
Arthur Thompson/Dana Talley/John Darrenkamp

Voice: Belén Amparán/Batyah Godfrey

Guardian: Mary Ellen Pracht/Joy Clements/Loretta Di Franco/
Eleanor Bergquist

Conductors: Karl Böhm/Erich Leinsdorf

Idomeneo
MOZART

Production by **Jean-Pierre Ponnelle**
Designed by **Jean-Pierre Ponnelle**
Lighting designed by **Gil Wechsler**
Premiere: October 14, 1982
Production made possible by a grant from the Lila Acheson Wallace Fund

Idomeneo: Luciano Pavarotti/Herman Malamood/William Lewis
Ilia: Ileana Cotrubas/Gail Robinson/Benita Valente
Idamante: Frederica Von Stade/Claudia Catania
Elettra: Hildegard Behrens/Kay Griffel
Arbace: John Alexander
High Priest: Timothy Jenkins/Charles Anthony
Voice of Neptune: Richard J. Clark
Women: Loretta Di Franco/Batyah Godfrey
Soldiers: Charles Anthony/James Courtney
Conductors: James Levine/Jeffrey Tate

L'Italiana in Algeri
ROSSINI

Production by **Jean-Pierre Ponnelle**
Designed by **Jean-Pierre Ponnelle**
Premiere: November 10, 1973

Isabella: Marilyn Horne/Nedda Casei/Lucia Valentini/Florence Quivar
Lindoro: Luigi Alva/Enrico Di Giuseppe/Douglas Ahlstedt/Rockwell Blake
Taddeo: Theodor Uppman/John Reardon/Sesto Bruscantini
Mustafà: Fernando Corena/Ara Berberian
Elvira: Christine Weidinger/Kathleen Battle/Betsy Norden
Zulma: Shirley Love/Nedda Casei
Haly: Gene Boucher/Allan Monk
Conductors: Gabor Ötvös/Henry Lewis/Nicola Rescigno

Lulu
BERG

Production by **John Dexter**
Designed by **Jocelyn Herbert**
Lighting designed by **Gil Wechsler**
Premieres: March 18, 1977 (first version);
December 12, 1980 (reconstructed version)
*Production a gift of Mrs. Edgar M. Tobin and
the Metropolitan Opera Club*

Lulu: Carole Farley/Alexandra Hunt/Teresa Stratas/Julia Migenes-Johnson
Schön: Donald Gramm/Franz Mazura
Jack the Ripper: Donald Gramm/Franz Mazura
Geschwitz: Tatiana Troyanos/Evelyn Lear
Alwa: William Lewis/Kenneth Riegel
Schigolch: Andrew Foldi
Ringmaster: Lenus Carlson
Rodrigo (Athlete): Lenus Carlson
Painter: Raymond Gibbs/Frank Little/Edward Sooter
Negro: Frank Little/Edward Sooter
Physician: Peter Sliker
Professor: Peter Sliker
Prince: Nico Castel/Robert Nagy
Manservant: Nico Castel/Robert Nagy
Marquis: Nico Castel/Robert Nagy
Wardrobe Mistress: Cynthia Munzer/Hilda Harris
Schoolboy: Cynthia Munzer/Hilda Harris
Groom: Hilda Harris
Theater Director: Richard Best/Ara Berberian
Banker: Ara Berberian
Journalist: John Darrenkamp
Waiter: James Courtney
Arts Patroness: Nedda Casei
Girl: Betsy Norden
Mother: Batyah Godfrey
Officer: Howard Sponseller
Clown: Abraham Marcus
Conductors: James Levine/Jeffrey Tate

Manon Lescaut
PUCCINI

Production by **Gian Carlo Menotti**
Designed by **Desmond Heeley**
Lighting designed by **Gil Wechsler**
Premiere: March 17, 1980
Production a gift of Mrs. Donald D. Harrington

Manon: Renata Scotto/Teresa Zylis-Gara/Carol Neblett/Mirella Freni/Adriana Maliponte
Des Grieux: Placido Domingo/Giuliano Ciannella/John Alexander/Ermanno Mauro/Vasile Moldoveanu
Lescaut: Pablo Elvira/Mario Sereni/Allan Monk/Brian Schexnayder/David Holloway/Lenus Carlson
Geronte: Renato Capecchi/Ara Berberian/Italo Tajo/James Courtney
Edmondo: Philip Creech/Kirk Redmann/Allan Glassman

Innkeeper: Mario Bertolino/William Fleck/Spiro Malas

Madrigalist: Isola Jones/Ariel Bybee/Claudia Catania/Diane Kesling/Gail Dubinbaum

Dancing Master: Andrea Velis/Nico Castel/Anthony Laciura/Joseph Frank

Sergeant: Julien Robbins/Andrij Dobriansky/Richard Vernon/John Darrenkamp

Lamplighter: John Carpenter/Dana Talley/Charles Anthony

Captain: Russell Christopher/Andrij Dobriansky

Conductors: James Levine/Thomas Fulton/Nello Santi

Otello
VERDI

Production by **Franco Zeffirelli**
Sets designed by **Franco Zeffirelli**
Costumes designed by **Peter J. Hall**
Premiere: March 25, 1972
Production a gift of Mrs. John D. Rockefeller, Jr.

Otello: James McCracken/Robert Nagy/Jon Vickers/Richard Cassilly/Placido Domingo/Edward Sooter

Desdemona: Teresa Zylis-Gara/Lucine Amara/Renata Tebaldi/Pilar Lorengar/Kiri Te Kanawa/Teresa Stratas/Katia Ricciarelli/Renata Scotto/Gilda Cruz-Romo/Atarah Hazzan/Margaret Price

Jago: Sherrill Milnes/Peter Glossop/Louis Quilico/Thomas Stewart/Cornell MacNeil/Anselmo Colzani

Emilia: Shirley Love/Jean Kraft

Cassio: Enrico Di Giuseppe/William Lewis/Leo Goeke/Raymond Gibbs/Frank Little/Giuliano Ciannella

Lodovico: Paul Plishka/Edmond Karlsrud/Raymond Michalski/James Morris/William Wildermann/Kurt Moll/Philip Booth/Gwynne Howell/Terry Cook

Montàno: Robert Goodloe/Clifford Harvuot/John Darrenkamp

Roderigo: Andrea Velis/Robert Schmorr/Charles Anthony

Herald: Raymond Gibbs/Gene Boucher/David Holloway/Arthur Thompson/Vernon Hartman

Conductors: Karl Böhm/Francesco Molinari-Pradelli/James Levine

Parade: An Evening of French Music Theatre

Production by **John Dexter**
Designed by **David Hockney**
Lighting designed by **Gil Wechsler**
Choreography for *Parade* by **Gray Veredon**
Incidental dances for *Les Mamelles de Tirésias* and
L'Enfant et les sortilèges by **Stuart Sebastian**
Premiere: February 20, 1981
Production a gift of Francis Goelet

Parade/SATIE

Harlequin: Gary Chryst

Columbine: Jane Muir/Antoinette Peloso

Vaudeville Lady: Kimberly Graves

Chinese Conjurer: Dave Roeger/Roberto Medina/Ricardo Costa

Elegant Woman: Pauline Andrey/Jean Anderson

Pierrot: Sam Cardea

Villain: Christopher Stocker/Jack Hertzog

Twins: Naomi Marritt/Antoinette Peloso/Martha Purl

Jazz Couples: Marcus Bugler/Nadine Tomlinson/Ricardo Costa/Lucia Sciorsci/Virgil Pearson-Smith/Suzanne Laurence/Joey Reginald/Ellen Rievman/Sarwat Kaluby/Della Weinheimer/Deanne Lay/Deborah Allton/Fredrick Wodin

Fat Ballerina: Roberto Medina/Gary Cordial

Commedia dell'arte: Vicki Fisera/Patricia Heyes/Jack Hertzog/Craig Williams

Conductor: Manuel Rosenthal

Les Mamelles de Tirésias/POULENC

Thérèse/Fortuneteller: Catherine Malfitano/Louise Wohlafka

Husband: David Holloway

Theater Manager: Allan Monk/Pablo Elvira/Brent Ellis/Brian Schexnayder

Presto: Christian Boesch/Darren Nimnicht

Lacouf: Joseph Frank

Gendarme: John Darrenkamp/Morley Meredith

Newspaper Seller: Jean Kraft

Journalist: Nico Castel

Son: James Atherton

Elegant Woman: Shirley Love/Claudia Catania

Large Woman: Geraldine Decker

Bearded Man: Andrij Dobriansky

Conductor: Manuel Rosenthal

L'Enfant et les sortilèges/RAVEL

Child: Hilda Harris

Mama: Isola Jones

Armchair: Julien Robbins

Louis XV Chair: Florence Quivar/Nedda Casei/Lucille Beer

Grandfather's Clock: David Holloway

Wedgwood Teapot: Robert Nagy

Chinese Cup: Claudine Carlson/Claudia Catania/Gail Dubinbaum

Fire: Ruth Welting/Myra Merritt

Shepherd: Claudine Carlson/Claudia Catania/Gail Dubinbaum

Shepherdess: Betsy Norden

Princess: Gail Robinson/Marvis Martin

Little Old Man: Joseph Frank

Black Cat: Gene Boucher

White Cat: Shirley Love/Emily Hastings

Tree: James Courtney

Dragonfly: Ariel Bybee/Diane Kesling

Nightingale: Gwendolyn Bradley

Bat: Therese Brandson

Squirrel: Florence Quivar/Nedda Casei/Barbara Conrad

Tree Frog: Andrea Velis

Screech Owl: Loretta Di Franco

Animals: Shirley Love/Nedda Casei/Robert Nagy/Richard Vernon/
Claudia Catania/Gail Dubinbaum/Emily Hastings/Anthony
Laciura/Norman Andersson

Conductor: Manuel Rosenthal

Peter Grimes
BRITTEN

Production by **Tyrone Guthrie**
Designed by **Tanya Moiseiwitsch**
Premiere: January 20, 1967
Production a gift of Mrs. Edgar M. Tobin

Peter: Jon Vickers/Robert Nagy/Richard Cassilly

Ellen: Lucine Amara/Phyllis Curtin/Heather Harper/Elisabeth
Söderström/Johanna Meier

Balstrode: Geraint Evans/Donald Gramm/Morley Meredith/Thomas
Stewart/Peter Glossop

Mrs. Sedley: Jean Madeira/Nancy Williams/Jean Kraft/Batyah
Godfrey

Auntie: Lili Chookasian/Geraldine Decker

Nieces: Mary Ellen Pracht/Lilian Sukis/Patricia Welting/ Christine
Weidinger/Betsy Norden/Alma Jean Smith/Louise Wohlafka

Hobson: Norman Scott/Louis Sgarro/Paul Plishka/Andrij
Dobriansky/Ezio Flagello/James Courtney

Swallow: Raymond Michalski/James Morris/Morley Meredith/
Richard Best/Jerome Hines

Boles: Paul Franke/Gabor Carelli/Charles Anthony/Robert Nagy

Adams: Robert Schmorr/James Atherton/Michael Best/Anthony
Laciura

Keene: Gene Boucher/Dale Duesing/John Darrenkamp/Darren
Nimnicht

Lawyer: William Mellow/Fawayne Murphy/Kent Cottam/John
Hanriot

Fisherwoman: Madelyn Coppock/Dorothy Shawn/Gail Leonard/
Lorraine Keane/Nadyne Brewer/Barbara Bystrom/Janet Wagner

Fisherman: Edward Ghazal/Frank Coffey/Donald Peck/Paul De
Paola/Merle Schmidt

John: Guy Curtis/John Allan/Steven Schachtel/Adam Wallach/
Kirk Peterson/Eugene Tournour

Conductors: Colin Davis/Sixten Ehrling/John Pritchard/David
Atherton

Porgy and Bess
GERSHWIN

Production by **Nathaniel Merrill**
Designed by **Robert O'Hearn**
Lighting designed by **Gil Wechsler**
Choreography by **Arthur Mitchell**
Premiere: February 6, 1985
*Production a gift of Mrs. Edgar M. Tobin, Robert L. B. Tobin, Mr. and
Mrs. John Pomerantz, Ira J. Hechler, and Wilmer J. Thomas, Jr.*

Porgy: Simon Estes/Robert Mosley

Bess: Grace Bumbry/Roberta Alexander

Sporting Life: Charles Williams/Bernard Thacker

Crown: Gregg Baker/Arthur Thompson

Clara: Myra Merritt/Marvis Martin

Jake: Bruce Hubbard/David Arnold

Serena: Florence Quivar/Veronica Tyler

Robbins: Donald Osborne/Vincent de Cordova

Jasbo: Joseph Joubert/Charles Darden

Mingo: John A. Freeman-McDaniels/Jerrod Sanders

Jim: Michael Lofton/Michael Smartt

Peter: Mervin Wallace

Lily: Priscilla Baskerville

Maria: Barbara Conrad/Elvira Green

Undertaker: Milton B. Grayson, Jr.

Frazier: John D. Anthony

Scipio: Clinton Chinyelu Ingram

Strawberry Woman: Isola Jones/Hillary Johnsson

Crab Man: Jay Aubrey Jones

Archdale: Gary Drane/Osie Hawkins

Detective: Larry Storch

Policeman: Andrew Murphy

Coroner: Hansford Rowe

Conductors: James Levine/William Vendice

I Puritani
BELLINI

Production by **Sandro Sequi**
Sets designed by **Ming Cho Lee**
Costumes designed by **Peter J. Hall**
Premiere: February 25, 1976

Elvira: Joan Sutherland

Arturo: Luciano Pavarotti

Riccardo: Sherrill Milnes/Cornelius Opthof

Giorgio: James Morris/Ezio Flagello

Enrichetta: Cynthia Munzer
Gualtiero: Philip Booth
Bruno: Jon Garrison
Conductor: Richard Bonynge

Tannhäuser
WAGNER

Production by **Otto Schenk**
Sets designed by **Günther Schneider-Siemssen**
Costumes designed by **Patricia Zipprodt**
Lighting designed by **Gil Wechsler**
Choreography by **Norbert Vesak**
Premiere: December 22, 1977

*Production a gift of the Fan Fox and Leslie R. Samuels Foundation
and the Metropolitan Opera Guild*

Tannhäuser: James McCracken/Richard Cassilly/Jess Thomas/
Edward Sooter/Gerd Brenneis

Elisabeth: Leonie Rysanek/Teresa Kubiak/Teresa Zylis-Gara/Eva
Marton/Johanna Meier

Wolfram: Bernd Weikl/Allan Monk/Håkan Hagegård

Venus: Grace Bumbry/Tatiana Troyanos/Dunja Vejzovic/Mignon
Dunn/Gwynn Cornell/Galina Savova

Hermann: John Macurdy/Kurt Moll/William Wildermann/Simon
Estes/Ara Berberian/Fritz Hübner

Walther: Misha Raitzin/Richard Kness/Timothy Jenkins/Robert
Nagy

Heinrich: John Carpenter/Charles Anthony/Paul Franke/Anthony
Laciura

Biterolf: Vern Shinall/Richard J. Clark/John Darrenkamp

Reinmar: John Cheek/William Fleck/Richard Vernon/James
Courtney

Shepherd: Kathleen Battle/Alma Jean Smith/Myra Merritt/Bill
Blaber/David Owen

Conductor: James Levine

Tristan und Isolde
WAGNER

Production by **August Everding**
Designed by **Günther Schneider-Siemssen**
Premiere: November 18, 1971
Production a gift of Mrs. John D. Rockefeller, Jr.

Tristan: Jess Thomas/Helge Brilioth/Jon Vickers/Spas Wenkoff/
Richard Cassilly/Manfred Jung/Edward Sooter

Isolde: Birgit Nilsson/Klara Barlow/Gwyneth Jones/Roberta Knie/
Hildegard Behrens/Johanna Meier

Kurwenal: Thomas Stewart/William Dooley/Walter Cassel/
Donald McIntyre/Richard J. Clark/Anthony Raffell

Brangäne: Mignon Dunn/Grace Hoffman/Irene Dalis/Michèle
Vilma/Tatiana Troyanos/Lorna Myers

Marke: John Macurdy/Giorgio Tozzi/Paul Plishka/Matti Salminen/
Aage Haugland/Martti Talvela

Melot: Rod MacWherter/William Lewis/Timothy Jenkins/Robert
Nagy

Sailor's Voice: Leo Goeke/Raymond Gibbs/Douglas Ahlstedt/Philip
Creech/Jeffrey Stamm/Kirk Redmann/Robert Nagy

Shepherd: Nico Castel/Charles Anthony/Paul Franke

Steersman: Louis Sgarro/Julien Robbins/James Courtney

Conductors: Erich Leinsdorf/James Levine

Die Zauberflöte
MOZART

Production by **Günther Rennert**
Designed by **Marc Chagall**
Premiere: February 19, 1967
Production a gift of Mrs. John D. Rockefeller, Jr.

Pamina: Pilar Lorengar/Judith Raskin/Teresa Zylis-Gara/Edith
Mathis/Adriana Maliponte/Lilian Sukis/Benita Valente/Anna
Moffo/Colette Boky/Carmen Balthrop/Leona Mitchell/Lucia
Popp/Gail Robinson/Kathleen Battle/Marvis Martin

Tamino: Nicolai Gedda/George Shirley/Luigi Alva/Peter Schreier/
Stuart Burrows/Leo Goeke/Kenneth Riegel/William Harness/Jon
Garrison/John Brecknock/Seth McCoy/David Rendall/David
Kuebler

Queen of the Night: Lucia Popp/Roberta Peters/Christine
Deutekom/ Colette Boky/Edda Moser/Rita Shane/Edita
Gruberová/May Sandoz/Zdzislawa Donat/Osceola Davis

Sarastro: Jerome Hines/John Macurdy/Bonaldo Giaiotti/Hans
Sotin/Ezio Flagello/Paul Plishka/Harald Stamm/Matti Salminen/
Martti Talvela

Papageno: Hermann Prey/Theodor Uppman/John Reardon/Donald
Gramm/Christian Boesch/Dale Duesing/Thomas Allen/Stephen
Dickson

Papagena: Patricia Welting/Loretta Di Franco/Judith Blegen/Gail
Robinson/Betsy Norden/Alma Jean Smith/Louise Wohlafka

Monostatos: Andrea Velis/Paul Franke/Nico Castel/Ragnar Ulfung/
James Atherton/Michael Best

Speaker: Morley Meredith/Walter Cassel/Donald Gramm/William
Dooley/Walter Berry/Edmond Karlsrud/Allan Monk/John
Shirley-Quirk/Donald McIntyre/Julien Robbins/Michael Devlin

First Lady: Jean Fenn/Mary Ellen Pracht/Clarice Carson/Jeannine
Altmeyer/Ellen Shade/Elizabeth Volkman/Alma Jean Smith/
Patricia Craig/Loretta Di Franco

Second Lady: Rosalind Elias/Shirley Love/Mildred Miller/Marcia
Baldwin/Jean Kraft/Ariel Bybee/Claudia Catania

Third Lady: Ruza Pospinov-Baldani/Nedda Casei/Belén Amparán/
Louise Pearl/Batyah Godfrey/Jean Kraft/Sheila Nadler/Isola Jones

Genii: Kevin Leftwich/Peter Herzberg/John Paul Bogart/David
Johnson/Gail Robinson/Judith Forst/Frederica Von Stade/Ivanka
Myhal/Loretta Di Franco/Carol Wilcox/Joseph Andreacchi/Adam
Klein/Steven Schachtel/William Newman/Baron Fitz-Gerald/